HAITI

Richard Frechette

HAITI

The God of Tough Places,
the Lord of Burnt Men

Transaction Publishers
New Brunswick (U.S.A.) and London (U.K.)

Library of Congress Catalog Number: 2009046758
ISBN: 978-1-4128-1420-1
Printed in the United States of America

Library of Congress Cataloging-in-Publication Data

Frechette, Richard.
    Haiti : the God of tough places, the Lord of burnt men /
    Richard Frechette.
        p. cm.
    ISBN 978-1-4128-1420-1 (alk. paper)
        1. Christianity--Haiti. 2. Haiti--Social conditions. I. Title.

BR645.H2F74 2010
277.29408'3--dc22

                                                    2009046758

Contents

Foreword

I suppose at some point, some librarian will categorize Fr. Rick Frechette's collection of essays as inspirational. If you ask this same clerk where you might find Hemingway's work, he or she will likely direct you to the section marked "Adventure Stories." Both observations are true, and yet could not be further from the truth.

While there is certainly inspiration to be found here, it comes at a cost that would crush most anyone I know. It would certainly have destroyed me; I barely survived reading some of these stories, let alone living them. If you think that an exaggeration, read ten pages at random and then come back and pick up here.

If you purchased this book—and I sincerely hope you did, because stealing it would seem wildly inappropriate—the chances are slim that you've experienced anything close to what is described on its pages. Haiti is a land of 80 percent unemployment, where the great majority of people somehow exist on between twenty-five cents and two dollars a day. It is a land of incredible contradictions and unfathomable daily occurrences. Events that in our world would be a subject of conversation for months, in Haiti often barely rate more than a wry mention. It is a world that embraces irony and humor and proverbs so colorful that a priest has to look over his shoulder twice before repeating them.

These contradictions aren't immediately evident to the wayward tourist. Like any slum in the world, drive past Wharf

Jérémie and all you can feel is pity. Get out and walk through these streets in the company of a man like *Pere Richard* and it is a remarkably different experience.

You steel yourself to absorb the horror of life in these despicable circumstances. You don't have to look for it; it floats in the open sewers and lives in the holes punched in tin roofs by tracer rounds fired by hovering soldiers. It blows with the dust that fills your lungs and the acrid stench that permeates your clothes.

But that's not what catches you off guard. What you weren't prepared to see, or feel, is the joy. It straightens the backs of women who take enormous pride in cleaning their eight by eight foot tin shacks, and of men who push carts bearing the carcasses of ancient automobiles. It spills from the empty buckets of women who walk miles in search of clean water, their laughter bouncing off the bullet-scarred walls of Cité Soleil. It shrieks from the mouths of pantsless children who bang a rusty barrel ring down the muddy road, or who dance with abandon just because they are wearing a pretty dress, despite the fact it is the same pretty dress they've worn for years, that their sister wore for years before that, that was picked out of a container of secondhand garments sent by well-meaning rich people. It shines in the faces of the grinning boys who sit on the roofs of their shacks, fishing in floodwater that drowned their grandparents and refuses to recede. What breaks your heart, and gives you hope, is the joy.

If you are lucky, like me, you get to leave before you see that joy ripped from those same hearts and hands.

If you stay … what is it that Yeats wrote? "Too long a sacrifice can make a stone of the heart." Few can live in a place like this and not surround themselves with walls as thick and tall as those that guard each house outside the slums.

That is what makes this collection even more remarkable. It is much more than a glimpse into a world that, while being an hour from American soil, is utterly foreign to us. This is a man standing before you, allowing you to stare unashamedly into the depths of his unguarded soul.

In these pages you will find a defiant man, sitting on a hot rock in the blistering sun, while worried gang members try and coax him into the shade. You find him chasing away hogs who would eat the bodies of men who themselves committed unthinkable atrocities. You find a man whose deep appreciation of the absurd helps him survive long nights negotiating the release of hostages—a man who buries as many children as he helps, but somehow still wakes up every day and helps more. And you will find a man who, lying on a concrete floor, stricken with dengue fever, still manages to inspire an army of lame and terminally ill patients to search the hills where Snake People hide the bodies of those whose only mistake was taking a shortcut home. He is a man who does daily battle with the cynicism and hatred that threatens to overwhelm his faith in mankind, and somehow draws lessons so surprising that they threaten to make an old atheist, like myself, believe in God.

This is a man who has broken his hands clearing rubble from a collapsed school, as children scratched at the underside of concrete slabs; a man who has seen too many friends and students and coworkers murdered, and who has himself at least twice narrowly escaped assassination—both times at the hands of desperate men he had raised since they were orphans. Both men whose lives he then tried to save.

Some of those things he writes about here. If you want to hear the others—like the attempts on his life, or how he freed the morgue workers who had been given life sentences for covering the wrong children's bodies with clean sheets—you will have to show up in Tabarre with enough red wine to share with Rick and his coworkers. You will probably have to wait for a while, as their days are long, administering the orphanage and making rounds at the pediatric hospital and the medical clinics, running the street schools, feeding thousands, delivering water, showing movies to the children of the slums, and the countless other things he and his Haitian colleagues do daily—including the most sinful waste of his time: raising money for all the above. Wait all night and he still may not tell you. However, you will leave with the certainty that you have met a man who finds God in the toughest places, and is a true friend to burnt men.

These are stories of humor and warmth and courage and hope. That said, they very well might sear the lining of your heart, as they did mine.

Paul Haggis
October, 2009

Introduction

The salmon, in an amazing display of instinct, fights its way upstream past hungry bears, through drowned branches, against crushing rocks and shearing currents, in order to arrive torn and exhausted at the place of its birth. The point of ending becomes the point of beginning, and life is born of sacrifice.

The autumn leaves blaze forth a dazzling array of colors, at precisely the moment when they are losing their life sap, and must soon cede to forceful winds, bitter cold, and the lessening of light. In this dramatic surrender to winter, life recedes with a show of glory, and then waits ever so patiently in the root. When light lengthens again and breezes become balmy, there will be an exuberant burst of all the forms and colors of life.

These are but two of many wonders which teach us the magnificent resilience that is the hallmark of life. This resilience often underlies tough realities, and requires that the promised glory await its season. What is revealed is a mysterious deep-seated determination for not just survival, but for full participation in and passion for life. The evidence is there for sacrifice, flare and gusto. Transcending the tough challenges brings metamorphosis and regeneration.

It is true for fish and for leaves. It is also true for people.

As a priest and a physician, I have known the body, mind, heart, and soul of many people, especially in the most anguishing circumstances of their lives. I have carried out my twin ministry mostly in settings of extreme poverty, social upheaval, and natural disasters. The backdrop of my profound encounters as priest and doctor has often been the crucible.

This personal experience of tough inner and outer places has been, naturally, both a loss and a gain. From privileged positions of comfort in the developed world, I have known firsthand lower economic and social realms of chaos, confusion, and tragedy. Yet, I have known this other world together with strangers who have become the best friends that one could hope for. We have faced together the most unspeakable tragedies, and yet also the most amazing resilience, bravery, longsuffering, and hope. This is the glory of the human being, paralleling the tattered and frayed victory of the salmon, and the astounding beauty of the autumn death rattle.

In the mention of friendship, it is also essential to note indebtedness to the spontaneous and gracious heroism of the absolute stranger. I have seen this amazing generosity many times. The right person appears at the right time and does the right thing and anonymously recedes. I once knew a missionary priest who was in solitary confinement, enduring harsh prison conditions and unbearable loneliness, after the Communist takeover in China. That experience soon had him completely disoriented, since he lived in the dampness and filth of an underground cell, deprived of light and thereby of a sense of time. He was alone in a miserable and perpetual darkness to ponder his destiny, to question God, and to long for his family and the slightest news of a friend, to suffer physical, emotional, and psychic anguish. He found a way to keep going, by exhausting himself during waking hours by endless repetition of prayer. Each time he was about to succumb to sleep, he would end his prayer by singing the traditional Catholic chant of vespers, in Latin, called the Magnificat.

The day came when this priest could take no more. He was physically, psychically and soulfully defeated. He refused all food and sought to waste away into diminishment, into the consoling embrace of death. His anonymous atheist guards, who had secretly admired his stamina and grown fond of his person and spirit, were distraught at the fact that he was withdrawn and apathetic. They tried to encourage him with words, but to no avail. They tried giving him extra bread, extra water, or some small treat. But he had receded far too deeply into despair and apathy to be able to respond to their gestures.

One day, when all else had failed, these two atheist guards who knew nothing of Latin, Christianity, or God, softly tried to sing to the defeated priest the alluring chant they had heard so many times from his lips. "Magnificat anima mea Dominum." In their deep desire to find some medicine for his soul, their emotional attempt to sing this chant broke through to the heart of the priest. A faint light dawned in his dark aloneness. He opened up to this light, born of friendship and solidarity from these two strangers, in full contradiction to their social mission. Fr. Justin found his way out of the inner darkness, and learned again how to survive in the outer, for the few more years that it would take to be liberated by the Red Cross.

Portents of mystery: the hardy fish, the dying leaf, the gracious stranger.

Haiti is a country of enormous natural beauty and extraordinary people. The following reflections are about events that took place during some very dark days in Haiti. They are not about Haiti. They are about any place, and any time, where people of any race and any class live out their lives and destinies in the tremendous stress of poverty. Poverty is a terrible and ongoing assault on human dignity. Yet, wherever and whenever the dignity of human person is assaulted and in peril, the human spirit seeks desperately to preserve what is most precious within it. It is an absolute wonder how people can find light and hope in the most despairing darkness. For we believers, this is the unfailing light of grace, ever present and faithful, and fiercely loyal to carrying out God's great work: renewing the face of the earth, renewing the embattled human heart.

The ancient human scourges of poverty, ignorance, sickness and violence still assault the dignity of our human family in too many places on earth, causing widespread humiliation of body, mind and spirit. Yet from the depths of this tragedy many people, with the help of God, and people like you and I, fight valiantly and are able to rise.

Fr. Richard Frechette, CP
Port-au-Prince
June 30, 2009

1

The God of Tough Places

(Second Sunday of Lent, the Transfiguration of Jesus)
March 6, 2004

Yesterday, nine of us went to Gonaïves, the epicenter of the revolution that just ousted former President Aristide. Our trip was without incident, except for the fact that, on arrival, those of us who sat in the back of the truck were absolutely covered with dust from the road. We were so dirty, that when we got to the cathedral we begged for a shower ... even if it had to be with holy water. Our need must have been evident, because we were almost pushed to water and buckets. It all happened so fast that Alfonso wound up getting a bath only because he happened to be standing next to me!

When five of us tried to make this same trip a month ago, it was a different story. The Sisters from Gonaïves had called me, because a ten-year-old boy was shot in the stomach, and his intestines were hanging out. He could be saved if we could get him to Port-au-Prince. We did our best to get to him, and we managed to get through three (of twenty) burning barricades. But after the third, we found ourselves out of the truck, arms in the air, guns to our heads. Although friends would probably never accuse me of being pious, I have always found the rosary to be extraordinarily helpful in such moments. We were released after a few Hail Mary's, and after explaining our mission. It was clear that we would never make it, and had to retreat to Port-au-Prince. But the gunmen had softened, and one of them even offered us his cell phone, in case we wanted to call the Sisters and tell them that we were "held up"!

I can't say we were fearless. But neither were we paralyzed by fear. Our strength came from trying to do the right thing. The gospel is very clear about what the right thing is. It's never hard to figure out. The gospel is just as clear about the price we may have to pay for doing the right thing … and this usually gives birth to a lot of second thoughts.

As we headed back home, we were pretty sad for the boy and our inability to reach him, and I kept questioning why the doors didn't open up for us to reach him. I have grown used to having lots of doors open through prayer. Late that night, when we were finally able to get through to the Sisters by phone, we learned that when we didn't show up, the Sisters ran their own barricades in the direction of Cap-Haïtien, looking blindly for help. They happened to find a visiting American surgeon, who operated and saved the boy's life. Suddenly it was clear to me that God didn't open the doors for us because they did not need to be opened. God did not need us in Gonaïves, thank you for trying, and found a rough way of turning us around before our zeal was converted into stubbornness and pride, leading us deeper into that bad night. Yesterday we had a nice reward in Gonaïves—we saw that little boy, healing, bright-eyed, and doing very well.

I see the Internet news keeps referring to Haiti as sliding into anarchy. We drove four hours yesterday, from Port-au-Prince to Gonaïves, without ever seeing a policeman or a soldier … or even a problem. To the contrary, everyone was trying to get on with a normal life. People were working in the rice paddies, pulling supplies to market, cutting sugar cane. Anarchy is far too exaggerated a word when referring to what is happening in Haiti. Yes, there are disastrous problems. Certain areas are politically hot and dangerous, demonstrations draw attacks, certain areas are notorious for looting and shooting, but these are localized and predictable. That is not anarchy. We have seen many times, over the past seventeen years, a "headless Haiti." But daily life goes on because the vast majority of people know their jobs and do them, even though for multitudes this results in an earning of less than a dollar a day.

The ride home from Gonaïves, at sunset, was spectacular. The large orange sun was setting into the turquoise ocean to our right. At the same moment, the full bluish moon was rising on our left. Our journey kept us positioned exactly between these two great lights of our heavens. They are God's gifts: one to govern darkness and the other to govern the day. I thought, "creation is showing us the meaning of this present moment in Haiti's history. We are caught between light and shadows, but we have the great lights to guide us." The lives of individuals and of nations keep tracing out this journey. We wander from darkness to light to darkness again, and sometimes we are in between. The important thing about darkness is to try to see in it, and the great lights have correlates in our mind's eye. The moon, unlike the sun, changes its shape and the intensity of its light a little bit every day, on its continuous journey from fullness to emptiness to fullness again. Its light is never constant, as is the light of the sun. In fact, the moon has no light. It reflects, imperfectly and in daily variation, the light of the sun. The same is true in our hearts. In the face of darkness (ignorance), the intensity and shape of light (understanding) is changing all the time. Light reveals itself in different ways, in the darkness.

Those who believe in God go through life trying to see how God is present in any moment, and what God's presence is saying. We look for light, and its message. This is harder to do in times of darkness. When things are especially rough, light can seem altogether absent. It is never totally absent, but it takes an eye trained in God's school (prayer) to recognize its shape and intensity.

As Ash Wednesday approached last week, I wrote about being called to bless the bodies of a number of poor people who were savagely killed after giving their life-savings to get a place on a boat heading for Miami. It was a poor, rickety boat that, for them, meant hope and deliverance. They were deceived, betrayed, and murdered, and their rotting bodies were washed up on the shore of a fetid slum. It was a very dark moment. My only thought, as I stood aghast, was how to bring some dignity to this nightmare. Focusing the attention of all present on a prayer for the dead, and for a better future, was all I could do. I carefully blessed each one with holy water. As I was leaving, I was approached by a fierce-looking stranger whose manner put me on my guard. Then, to my great surprise, he thanked me for coming to pray and said how important it is that goodness not perish. Suddenly, in that darkness, there was an amazing light, just like in the Transfiguration of Jesus. "Lord, it is good for us to be here." Yes, it was absolutely good to be there, and to see this man's faith and hope shine brightly.

Let me get the worse things over with. I also mentioned in that reflection that I was told that when I came back, I would see the pigs eating those bodies. I did go back to Wharf Jérémie, as I always do on Wednesdays. But I had no intention of going to the shoreline where the bodies were. I had already offered, several times, to bury them—but it is interference with the State to do so. However, even without intending to go near the shoreline, fate had another plan. There, on the very road to the wharf, I had to stop the truck because of a bunch of pigs blocking our way. As I approached, I was horrified at what I saw, with my own eyes. We jumped out of the truck and chased the pigs away with stones. This was a different body. There were many of them scattered in the area—bodies of people who had been killed while looting the nearby port. We tried once again to bring dignity to what can only be described as a scene right out of hell. Alfonso, Sister Lorraine, Malherbe, and I rolled what was left of the pig-eaten body into a white body bag, chased the pigs off again, and once more offered prayers for the dead, and for a better future. I have heard Haiti referred to as a failed state. In the face of things like this, that is the understatement of the year.

To complicate the darkness even more, I soon learned that the man whose remains we tried to honor was one of the three men who betrayed and killed the people in the boat. I could feel welling up within me the urge to rejoice in such a bad ending for him. But this is not God's way, nor is it the way of light. I could only shake my head, so rattled by the strength of the culture of death, at the ferociousness of evil and how it devours those who enter into it. I remember in Dante's Inferno, every punishment fit the sin precisely, and they were pretty frightening images. This man's sin and his punishment were well matched, but this is so not because of the nature of God, but rather because of the nature of evil. I thought of God's warning to Cain: the power of evil crouches at the door like a lion, eager to destroy and devour those who enter into sin.

The vast slums of Port-au-Prince are pretty rough places. Yet they are home for hundreds of thousands of people. Most of these are children. If people are there, God is there fully there too.

After we chased off the pigs and offered our prayer, I raised my head and saw three powerful things. I saw the wind blow the hat off or a woman, and a child run barefoot through the muck to get it for her. I saw a home-made kite, fashioned from twigs and old bags, and many pieces of old string joined together, soaring high above the filth. And I saw the children running to meet us, squealing in joy, as we approached them with our music, our food, and our books. Yes, this darkness is filled with countless twinkling stars. They are called children. I think of our home for orphan children in the mountains of Kenscoff. How many people remark it is like an oasis! How we have seen children from places like this recapture their childhood there! But there must be a way to help these children cling to their childhood, even in the face of brutish realities and hellish images. The blessings we have at our orphanage—security, beauty, peace, food, medicines, books—surely must overflow and reach here. Why not? Here is some great advice from Sister Mary Alban, a Canadian Sister of St. Joseph, who has been in Haiti for years. "If it's old and ugly, paint it a bright color. If it's barren, plant a flower. If it's broken, glue it together or even make something new with the pieces. If its garbage, make compost. If they're fighting, sing a song. If they're sick, sit with them on the bed. If they are hungry, make soup."

Guess who is parading into Wharf Jérémie with paints, plants, glue, guitars, medicine, food, and books. We are. And we will do our best to give these children a childhood.

On our way to the poor areas this past week, every day we made an extensive drive around Port-au-Prince in order to look for the wounded. Guardian angels in the form of absolute strangers detoured us away from areas of shooting, parted chanting mobs to let us pass through (as Moses parted the Red Sea), and signaled to us different people in distress. I will tell you about one of them. A man was pushing what we thought was a dead woman in a wheelbarrow. We thought he was heading to the morgue of the general hospital, already overflowing with 200 rotting bodies. We stopped to talk with him, and saw that the woman was not dead. She had been shot in the head yesterday, in the shoot-outs in the capital, and he had been wheeling all around the city ever since, looking in vain for help. She was nearly dead, and beyond saving. But we took her to a private hospital and paid all the bills for the best care they could give her. A visiting doctor chided me: she needs the home for the dying, not a hospital. I replied, "I am not putting her in the hospital for her, I am putting her in the hospital for her husband." To me it was very important that her husband see that someone did everything possible for his wife, against all odds. Why? Because for me, he was the brightest light in Port-au-Prince that day, giving us an incredible witness of fidelity and love.

The holy ancient writers tell us that the purpose of the Transfiguration, when Christ's face shone out as radiant as the sun, was to strengthen the apostles for the terrible darkness of Calvary, that would come before the Resurrection. It didn't work. Most of Christ's followers, including the first pope, ran off in terror, just as most of us would have done and would do today. But that doesn't make the meaning of the Transfiguration any less real. Every word of the Bible is written for today, not yesterday. Beneath the most ordinary, or the most difficult, or the most brutish situations of life there is a light for us to see, and it bears a wondrous message of God's love. It is always there, as a gift, when we pray for the right eyes to see it.

Fr. Richard Frechette, CP

2

The Lord of Burnt Men

April 15, 2004

The prophet Isaiah startles us with the image of a man, a servant of God, who is so disfigured that he doesn't even look human. Absolutely lacking any beauty or charm to win our hearts, we even avert our gaze rather than look him, who seems so "accustomed to sorrow and acquainted with grief."

I know another such man. He was already acquainted with the bitterness of life in impoverished Haiti, before a charlatan completely disfigured him by pouring boiling lye on his head, as a cure for epilepsy.

Just yesterday, Daniel begged me to let him leave the poor house that serves as a makeshift hospital, so he could go home. This pitiful man, blind from searing acids, his head crowned with open wounds, wants to go "home"—where the filth, violence, heat, and lack of even clean water to wash his sores will certainly spell his death. But home is always home, and has its soothing lure.

Daniel told me that he was being assailed by demons at night, and was sure that if he stayed any longer he would either lose his mind or die. Although he certainly needs medicine to calm him and therapy for his twisted heart, Daniel's image of demons alerts us to his profound spiritual crisis. The meaning of his life has been mercilessly disfigured. He was betrayed by a "healer." His precious life, his dreams, his hopes, and even the face and eyes that mirror his soul were all fuel for fiery lava. Now he gropes in darkness to understand what life means, and who God is, when wickedness has made you a monster. He strives to know, in the words of Thomas Merton, the Christ of burnt men.

Daniel searches deeply for answers while in the worse possible state of soul. Just as it is true that holiness is the "wholeness" of personal integrity (and this wholeness buffers us against dangerous spiritual forces), it is also true that disintegration and brokenness make us vulnerable and sensitive to the forces of evil. That is what makes the last temptation of Christ, and the present temptation of Daniel, unspeakable.

Daniel talks of demons during the holy days of Easter, the proclamation of the mystery that a crucified Christ, who had descended even into the bowels of hell, is now gloriously alive. This truth is the very root of the Christian heart and must have practical and tangible meaning. Love will not, love cannot, give up on Daniel. Not our love, nor the love of God.

We hope a cornea transplant will help Daniel's remaining eye to see again the light of day. We hope skin grafts will take root on his naked skull. But mostly we pray that Daniel might have the same inner dialogue with the risen Christ that the risen Christ had with his chosen ones. They had locked themselves in a room and groped in fear when He came to them, showed them His wounds transformed, and gave them the peace that surpasses all understanding.

Fr. Richard Frechette, CP

3

The Transfiguration of Barnabas

August 6, 2004

Dear Friends,

Today, the Catholic liturgical calendar marks the feast of the Transfiguration of Christ on Mount Tabor. I have always liked this day, both because celebrations of radiance are appealing, and because it takes place in my favorite month. August is the month my mother and I celebrate our birthdays, and has often been a lazy month of rest and celebration.

For a moment, on Mount Tabor, a few privileged apostles were allowed to see what was under the surface of the ordinary day. The face of Christ glowed like the sun, revealing that the apparent ordinariness of life is charged with the splendor of God. Yes, the vision of that splendor is blunted by the woundedness of sin and we are often blinded to it, but it is there for us to see at special moments of grace. In particular, we are told by wise and holy people that the apostles were granted this special vision because they would need the memory of this experience to see them through the dreadful days of Christ's passion.

Three nights ago, as we were driving to the orphanage after a long and hot day of work, we came upon a man sitting on the road in the market at Fermathe. He seemed baffled and dazed. He was vomiting, and his body was twisting with the movements of a snake. People from the town were giving him milk to drink. I thought he was just drunk, and I was tempted to pass by, but I didn't. The quick story from the local people was that he ate two bagfuls of rat poison. Since I did not have any antidotes for poison with me, nor activated charcoal to try to absorb what was still in his stomach, we put him in the truck and raced to the nearby small hospital. There was no doctor there. So we raced him along the harrowing road, about 7 kilometers to the orphanage, where I called ahead so that oxygen, IV fluids, activated charcoal, and other treatments would be waiting for us.

The man's name is Barnabas. To spare you a lot of the story, I will simply say that it was soon clear that his snakelike movement's were not from the poison. Barnabas, who is 43 years old, told me he has been like that since he was 26. I suspect he has Huntington's, or a similar neurological disease. Barnabas' wife left him for a normal man, and he lives in Cap-Haïtian with his two high school age children, whom he can no longer afford to get through school. Tired of his advancing illness, tired of the gawks and comments of strangers, ashamed that he can't hold anything long enough in his hands to be able to hold down a job so he can get his children through school, he decided to take a bus to Port-au-Prince and to take his life. He decided to do this far from his family and from anyone he knows, to spare them the shame and despair of his ending.

I asked Barnabas if he really wanted to die, and there was a flood of tears. They were tears from the soul of someone who found a compassionate ear, which is also a bridge of bonding and a relief from loneliness. No, Barnabas did not want to die. Barnabas was in an inner hell and did not know there was still a heaven, until a light shown upon him through a simple act of kindness.

Barnabas now has a job with us. There are many ways he can help us. We will see to it that his children finish school. We will find the best medicines available in the United States to lessen his writhing movements and help slow the course of his devastating illness. And now he will have friends to the end, even though it can be a bitter end. We can try to make it at least bittersweet. As I said in reference to today's feast, the apostles were granted this special vision because they would need the memory of this experience to see them through dreadful days. Our religion is always enormously practical.

After the transfiguration, life became difficult once again. Maybe Hollywood would write the script so that moments of transfiguration would be last moments, but God has a different idea. Jesula, Daniel and now Barnabas are faced with many challenges and their full humanity can make them very heavy to themselves and to us. There are people who have told me that I should have rewritten some of those scripts, that I should be more willing to let people die. The idea of assisting suicide, or of determining who should be helped to live and who should be left to die, are hot and controversial topics in our world today. It is just that I have not yet come across someone who said to me, "Thanks for offering help, but I really would just rather die." I am waiting for such a moment, and its accompanying wisdom.

On another note, in the areas of flooding, we have found donations of seed for about 100 people to replant their gardens and we are in the process of building the first five simple houses for those who have lost their homes. Sister Philomena, on her own, has raised the money to build an additional three!

On this feast of radiance, we offer our prayers for you and your families.

Sincerely,
Fr. Richard Frechette, CP

4

A Tale of Two Tragedies

September 25, 2004

One week ago today, the funeral at the orphanage of our dear little Immacula coincided with the great flood that destroyed the town of Gonaïves. Only now do I have the courage to write about both.

Immacula had been with us since she was a small child. Her mother and her sister had died of AIDS, and she was also infected with that dread disease. Immacula was a child who never thrived, who always had sufferings from sickness, which she fought with full force. In her young years, when only a single drug was recommended for people with AIDS, we bought it for her at huge expense. Some years later, we started her on the newly recommended triple therapy, which continued to her death. Even though the good medicines only helped her in a moderate way, Immacula lived a dozen years longer than she would have otherwise. Those dozen years were truly good years, in fact precious years, of fullness of life. That is why so many of our staff kept watchful vigil at her bedside during her final weeks of decline, at which time Immacula told Adele that she knew she was dying, though she really wished she could live.

Of the hundreds of children who have lived with us, some remain anonymous to me because I am mostly with them when they are crowded together at mass or community gatherings. But over the years, a good number of have made their way into my mind and heart, because of sudden and endearing moments. In Immacula's case, I remember vividly a Christmas play after Mass many years ago, and how Susana had coaxed the wee Immacula into singing for us with her deep, husky voice. She took the microphone and sang a very sweet song about peace. The tune was haunting, and the chorus ended with the words "and that's when peace will finally come back to us." I remember it especially well because Immacula was herself so moved by the song, that she started to cry, and Susana had to come and take her away from the microphone in a warm, misty eyed embrace.

Immacula's death and funeral were part of a death duet, because parallel to our dance with her death, a hundred miles away, another tragedy was unfolding. As Immacula's soul was in the throes of being released from its body, a storm named Jeanne was in the throes of releasing oceans of water onto the mountaintops above Gonaïves. The two separations were soon completed. As Immacula's soul left her body, so Jeanne's floodwaters broke free from the clouds and raced along mountain paths to the sea. As we prepared the lifeless body of Immacula for burial in great sorrow, we called all the children together to pray over her body, and we marched in long procession from the small chapel to the outdoor altar near the cemetery. At the same time, far off in the hills, the massive waters of Jeanne raced down the ravines in their own disordered procession. Lifeless in front of me, I blessed Immacula's body with the holy water and the gentle prayer: "as you died with Christ in the waters of Baptism, may you now share with Him the joy of the resurrection." Meanwhile, non-baptismal waters of destruction descended upon the unaware people of Gonaïves, with deadly force.

"Lord have mercy, Christ have mercy, Lord have Mercy", our Mass continued. These same words of pleading were filling the panicked streets of Gonaïves, as the floodwaters crashed through the town.

As I placed the gifts of bread and wine on the altar of sacrifice, another missionary priest, who had once worked in the violent lands of Cambodia and Laos, was now living out the final sacrifice of himself in Haiti. He had once faced a firing squad, and was given a last-second miraculous reprieve. He had also survived prison, and a grenade explosion. For the past 40 years he worked in Gonaïves, taking care of people with leprosy. Now in his golden years, he lived on the property of the Sisters of Mother Theresa, offering mass and caring for the sick. Our friend Sister Abha, who had opened the home for the dying in Port-au-Prince together with Mother Theresa some 25 years ago, had been recently transferred from Port-au-Prince to Gonaïves. An older man, who had already lost one limb to leprosy, lived with the old missionary priest in his little house, and Sister Abha attended to them often. As the floodwaters poured into their courtyard, the sick were rushed to the chapel, which was on the highest ground. The Sisters returned to the convent, trying to reach their priest on the way. But they could not approach his house because of the torrents. Inside their convent, the floodwaters also began to rise so fast, they soon poured into the house through the windows.

The Offertory: "In Immacula's memory, may the Lord accept this sacrifice at our hands, to the praise and Glory of God's name, for our good and the good of all the Church." The waters of the flood entered the house of the old missionary, and the life of this remarkable priest came to its end. May the Lord also accept the sacrifice at his hands.

I held the precious bread high in the air above Immacula's body. "This is my Body, which is given up for you."

The consecration was completed, I held the body and blood of Christ above the altar. The Sisters, meanwhile, were making different use of their altar. They climbed atop it in an effort to stay alive, above the waters filling their house. Their white habits were stained by dark mud, and the waters rose higher still. They could not escape the rising waters. They prepared themselves, fearfully, for death. Immacula's mass continued: "Deliver us O Lord from every evil, and grant us peace in our day. Keep us free from sin and protect us in all anxiety, as we await in joyful hope the coming of our Savior, Jesus Christ."

One by one, the children filed passed Immacula's body. "Body of Christ." "Amen." Wide eyes. No tears yet. The children have a way of shielding themselves from the harsh realities that already had marked their young and tender lives.

By a merciful act of God, as the Sisters were about to drown, their perimeter wall gave in and collapsed from the force of the waters. It was carried off with the torrent. The water inside the convent made a rapid descent, equalizing with the lower water level on the open streets and fields. The Sisters were saved, safe on their altar. And the waters rose no higher.

"The mass is ended, go in peace."

In the cemetery, the choir of children was singing as we lay Immacula in her grave. With this sweet music and tender scene, the children could contain themselves no longer. They had known Immacula for years and loved her as a dear friend, and dreadful wailing and frantic cries began to fill the air from scores of children. Sarah, Gena, Sister Lorraine, Adele, Sister Ancie and so many others gathered as many children in their arms as they could. It was dreadful. Who could not weep at the sound, the sight, the pain? But that lament could never come near to the wailing and screaming taking place in Gonaïves, where there was no solid ground on which anyone could stand, to gather the desperate and the drowning into their arms. Children were washed cruelly away from their desperate mothers, humble homes were uplifted and destroyed, dead horses and cows, and dead grandmothers and uncles floated in the mud toward the sea. And a small baby boy in a basket, placed in it by his drowning mother. He was later found alive, and given to us, and we named him Moses, for he was also drawn out of the waters.

"In paridisum perducant te angeli…."

"May the angels lead you into paradise."

The traditional chant for the dead became the lamentation of two thousand desperate souls.

In the cemetery, the children could not be consoled. I started to gather the crying children one by one, placing into their hands the bowl of holy water, asking them to bless the grave. One by one they took it. They approached the grave with heavy sobs, but somehow found peace and power in this blessing. They blessed Immacula's grave with holy water, an outward sign of God's grace, and they blessed it again with their tears, an outward sign of their grace. Slowly the level of wailing descended.

And slowly the waters descended in Gonaïves.

The funeral over, we went at once to Gonaïves. We would go in solidarity, to show our concrete friendship and care, and to see what help we could offer.

Five hours of dreadful roads. We arrived after sunset. To get into the city we had to drive through a lake that had once been rice fields. Our headlights were completely underwater, and only darkness and dark waters were before us, waters that rose to our doors. Two guides stood on our sideboards, guiding us along so we would not fall off the underwater road, as had many overturned trucks and buses, which lay at our right and our left. They looked like huge buoys, marking the two-kilometer crossing. Gonaïves was dark and desolate and in ruins. There were no signs of people, at least not at night. We plowed through the waters, the garbage, the broken city until we arrived at the Sisters. They came out to greet us … muddy but happy to see friends, recounting in detail their ordeal. It was late … everything covered with mud, we had no choice but to sleep in the truck on the only clear patch of land we could find.

In the early morning we celebrated mass together. It was a mass of thanksgiving for life, a mass of remembrance for the victims, a mass for the priest who had died, and a mass to beg God for help. After mass, the Sisters gave us canned breakfast from army rations that they had stored, and some eggs and bread that had been stored high. We made lists of what would be needed from Port-au-Prince, and we went off to the city again to look for the families of our friends.

Wandering through the streets in water to our waist, as dead animals floated by, and where people washed muddy clothes in the even muddier water that engulfed us, it would be impossible to describe the extent of the disaster. Everything was destroyed to a height of 15 feet. Electric lines dipped into the waters around us. People greeted us from the roofs on which they were huddled together with whatever belongings they could salvage, on roofs which had saved their lives. They called down to us "be careful the white man doesn't fall into the canals. He doesn't know where they are on the side of the road. He is wet enough."

"Thank you! Ki gen nou ye? How are you?"

"Nou pa pi mal…. We are not bad. When you still have your life you have everything."

While the roads were filled with underwater garbage, furniture, and rocks, the courtyards were filled with underwater mud. As we entered the courtyard of the house of one friend's mother, our sandals were sucked off by the deep mud with every step. The body of an old woman was apparent, buried face down in the mud. We uncovered enough mud from her enough to know it was not his mom, and we stopped to pray for her. We could not remove her body simply because there was absolutely no place to put her. And we would never have been able to carry her back through the waters, two miles back to the truck. We trudged further into the city, looking at belongings piled high on the roofs, drying in the sun. The people had begun the arduous task of digging six feet of mud out of their houses.

With gratitude to God for the safety of the Sisters and of so many others, and moved by the concern for us shown by many strangers on their rooftops, and very inspired by the great spirit shown by those already starting to reshape their lives, we headed back to Port-au-Prince, so that we could start organizing more serious help. The same help we continue to offer in Thiote since the terrible floods of last May. Everything is needed. Everything. Clothes, water, cots, food, medicine, seeds for replanting, cement for rebuilding, shovels for digging through the mud. Everything is needed, but the day is young ... and when you still have your life you have everything.

Fr. Richard Frechette, CP

5

On the End of the World
(and Other Chances to Renew the
Face of the Earth)

November 17, 2004

Last Sunday, we entered into the last fortnight of the Catholic liturgical year. We have relived, for 50 weeks, the story of our salvation, for the purpose of releasing its power, concretely, into the days of 2004. With only a handful of days left before the grand finale, the proclamation of Christ as Victor over all the forces of the shadow world, which would destroy life and love, we find a big surprise. We enter this fortnight, just about at the end of our journey, with troubling words from Christ. We are told of darkness and trials, of great battles, of such destruction that not one stone will be left on another ... not even in the Temple. What happened? We thought He won out over death?

He did. But He won only to make our winning possible. Christ's victory did not exempt us from the struggle. To the contrary, from the minute we are born until the second we die, we are intimate participants in the drama between good and

27

evil, between life and death, and our choices make all the difference in the world. We constantly relive our liturgical year for the empowerment of remembrance, so that our choices are influenced by the very heart of God. "I set before you good and bad, life and death. Choose life!"

There is nothing imaginary about the apocalypse, the dramatic and showy display of chaos. On November 2nd, we gathered outside of Port-au-Prince, as we always do, at the killing fields and common grave of the untold number of nameless poor, who died during 2004. Too poor even to be buried. Their bones, strewn about, speak of apocalypse. They are dumped there without dignity, without tenderness, without hope of another life. We gather there to repair the damage done to them: we proclaim their dignity, at that place, by celebrating for them the exalted rite of the Mass. Many of them, when sick, were under our care. We remember their lives with tenderness, we commend them to God with the hope of a better and eternal life. This is what I mean when I say that our liturgical year empowers us to make grace present, concretely, in our world.

It is not a coincidence that the Church asks us, in November, not only to reflect on the Last Days, but also to offer concrete acts of charity for the dead. Prayers, fasting, graveside visits. Just as the suffering of Christ made salvation possible for us, in a mysterious way our efforts and sufferings can help other people find theirs. We are encouraged to offer our works, our trials, our sufferings to God in union with those of Christ so that they might be redemptive. Our Church offers us the intuition that many of the dead still need our solidarity in order to find their deliverance. (Our Pope has been asking repeatedly, in recent years, for people to pray for him after his death.) For the dead, it is literally true that not one stone is left on another. The dead have lost everything in the world as we know it.

Nor can our charity for the dead stop with spiritual works of charity. We have to work so that no one is ever thrown into a mass grave again. Everyone should be buried with dignity, tenderness, and hope. This is a most worthy human goal. We have overwhelming numbers of destitute dead. We see the death of 250 children a year at our own hospital, not to mention at all the other places where we work. A team of young adults who have grown up in our orphanage have formed a "ministry of Tobit." One by one, they are starting to bury our dead. They make the coffins, they dig the graves, they bring the family to the rented ground for burial and prayer (yes, rented graves, until we can afford to buy a cemetery). It makes all the difference in the world to the family, as you can imagine. It is a simple act that gives a psychological and spiritual rock to stand on, in the face of the death of their child. This is grace taking hold, concretely, in the days of 2004.

There is nothing imaginary about the apocalypse. We have seen beheaded corpses in Port-au-Prince. I read recently in the *New York Times* that this barbaric act is making a comeback not only in Iraq and Haiti, but also in any number of countries around the world.

Twice during the past month our medical team had to drive into violent areas at night, to bring out the sick and wounded in order to save their lives. Both times, it was bad people who made sure that we got in and out without our truck being burned, or smashed, or worse. It is amazing how many bad people still have an instinct for good, and if given a chance, participate in goodness. Human history is full of stories of people whose destructive behavior comes from being convinced by others, often by their own leaders, that their warrior behavior is for a noble cause. A lot of the bad people are children—completely misguided and manipulated children. How important it is to put good and right ideas in their head, to use their minds instead of wasting them. A number of young adults who grew up in our orphanage are forming clusters of little schools to get these kids off the street, away from bad influences, and into more human and life-giving friendships. One group is called "Companions of St. Gabriel." Another, "Companions of St Anne," and so on. So far, they have organized schools for 400 street children. Our goal is to have 1000 street children in schools by the end of the new year of grace, 2005. When bad people follow good instincts, and are encouraged to do so, grace is breaking in on apocalypse. Then one sees clearly that it is not so much that a bad person was converted to goodness, but rather that the person whose goodness was perverted is back on the right track. Grace is really something. And how proud we are that our huge home and school for orphan children, now running for 17 years, has produced young people who are trying to renew the face the earth.

There is nothing imaginary about the apocalypse. Violence and natural disasters are seeing to it that not a stone is left standing on another in many places in the Middle East, in parts of the flood areas of Gonaïves and Thiote, in Afghanistan and Falluja. Even the natural disasters, in many cases, are caused by such violence toward the earth as deforestation and destruction of natural habitats. Someone just mailed me a load of seeds to plant in Gonaïves. Grace insists on breaking in on apocalypse.

Speaking of Gonaïves, we have received three children from there. Moses is eight months old, and was found miraculously alive floating in the water, by UN soldiers. His family is presumed dead. We call him Moses because his name, like that of his famous namesake, means in Hebrew "drawn out from the waters." He is chubby and beautiful. Then there is Guenson. I guess he's about ten. His last memory of his family is his grandmother putting him safely in the branches of a tree, and then watching her disappear with the waters. Then there is Vilina. She was the most traumatized from the loss of her whole family, but she is starting to come out of herself, thanks to Sister Loraine and our hospital staff. The three of them are witnesses to the incredible resilience of spirit, which we celebrate throughout our liturgical year.

Wherever not even one stone was left atop another, we have been piling and cementing stones again. We have rebuilt homes for 25 families in Thiote. One of the young men who grew up in our orphanage oversaw this whole project. And this week we are finalizing the details to help 40 families in Gonaïves have a home again. If our faith is not concrete and practical, it is, as St. Paul says, thoroughly lifeless.

Forgive the personal note, but it has an important message. Since last February, we have had a major revolution and two disastrous floods. And since August I have had both malaria and dengue fever. You can imagine that even someone people considered strong, and who usually feels very strong, also has his limits. The dengue put me flat on a mat on the floor, depressed and exhausted, covered with rashes and wet with fevers. Dengue is known for causing depression. Then again, so is life. The floor helped me a lot because it was cool against the fevers. And the hardness of the floor protected my aching bones from sudden movements. To make it worse, while on my sick bed, I got three pieces of terrible news. A friend, Ti Maurice, was dying in his hovel in Cité Soleil and wanted me to go see him, which was impossible. Then news came that one of the young men teaching our street children, was killed brutally in the gunfire of Port-au-Prince. This was followed by the news that Daniel, the subject of a previous letter of mine, had died. Daniel had suffered disfiguring acid burns on his head and face from a witch doctor who had used the acid to try to exorcise him during an epileptic seizure. In any case, the pathetic Daniel died in a gutter in Port-au-Prince.

Of all the chaos wrought by apocalypse, chaos of the spirit is the worst—that awful feeling that not one stone is standing on another inside of yourself. I wondered as I lay on the floor if there was anything about life even worth getting up for again, even if I could get up. That is a sickness. I knew it was self-pity to think that way. I knew I was nowhere near as sick as my hundreds of patients, and my life nowhere near as dire as theirs. But the cure came to me. So many people came to see me, standing at the foot of my mat, so obviously sad that I was sick. And I voiced to some of them my inner thoughts, and I heard from some good advice, and from others kind words, and from others still some chiding, and from some very strange ideas indeed … but from all of them I heard, very clearly, friendship. Our community heals us. I am fine again, and I feel strong, thanks to love.

I was told later by a friend that it was revealed to her in prayer that my illness was not just about a mosquito. The suffering I went through, on a deeper level, was helpful for Daniel's final deliverance after his tormented ending. I don't know if it is true. I do know our Church teaches that our suffering can be redemptive. I also know that if it is true, I would gladly have lain on that mat for a year for Daniel, if it could have repaired any of the damage that chaos had inflicted on him.

And so our liturgical year is about to end. It's time to "stand up and be counted" and face the hard truth about life, with gospel in hand and heart. No need to fear. The whole year starts again on the first Sunday of Advent. We will hear the sweet announcement that God is coming to us, into our reality, into our flesh. And then we will have 52 weeks to relive the story and release its power, and we will have a chance to do this again and again and again, until we get it right. Nothing to fear. The power is in us, all of us. Big or small, smart or slow, rich or poor, sick or well. The power is in all of us. It's in our hearts. It's called love.

Fr. Richard Frechette, CP

6

The Tiny Mustard Seed and the Ferocious Gates of Hell

March 20, 2005

As a priest, I think I know a little bit about heaven and hell. As a doctor, I think I know a little bit about life and death. But certainly this past season of winter, which ends today, taught me a lot more than I knew about any of them, especially about hell. I am glad to see winter end, and it's not because I am sick of snow.

I suppose it isn't surprising that the dead of winter would teach us about death. It also isn't surprising that the cold and darkness of winter would teach us about hell. In Dante's *Divine Comedy*, hell is presented as a frozen darkness, devoid of flame and heat. Fire is too representative of wisdom, of warmth and Spirit, to find a place in hell.

For those of us who live in the northern half of the world, winter begins on December 21st, with what is called the winter solstice. Solstice literally means the sun stands still. It stands still as far away from us as it will ever get, leaving us with the days of the least light. The sun stands still in order to turn

35

around and, thankfully, start coming back toward us. If it didn't, if it continued its journey away from us, the whole planet and every living creature on it, would perish in frozen darkness in a very short time. Yes, thank God the sun stops, and considers us, and returns to us. At the same time as it is turning, the Christian Church celebrates the great feast of Christmas. This is not a coincidence. Christ, the true light of the world, begins a journey toward us that will save from perishing in the frozen darkness of sin. His considering us, his turning toward us, will save us from hell. Nature teaches us clearly about grace, the sun teaches us about the Son.

In the beginning of the Bible, we see that creation is God's deliberate act of controlling chaos by setting forceful boundaries. Boundaries between light and darkness, between land and water, between good and evil. Unbelievable horrors, like tsunami and Shoah, show us what is at stake when boundaries disappear. Hell is in the business of trying to destroy all boundaries. And resisting hell is about fighting to restore them.

One of our deceased priests, who was a bit of a character, would give out his business card liberally. It said:

Fr Camillus Barth, CP.
Working to beat hell!

When I was young, this thought made me chuckle. Today, it makes me shudder.

As the solstice approached, so did the gates of hell. My work takes place with people very much disgraced by abject poverty and brutal violence. It doesn't often seem like there is a whole lot of light around. The light is surely not in the crushing reality in which the people are born and die. But it is in their eyes and hearts, and it glows in ways that give tremendous witness to God's reign.

At the solstice, a young man named Joseph made the bad mistake of wanting to cut 45 minutes off a trip to see his family, by driving through an area of Port-au-Prince well known to me and my roaming medical team, called "New Road." There he met his death in a savage way. More savage still, his body was left in his car to rot. Neither police nor UN soldiers would go to the area. Joseph was a graduate of a famous American university. He was working at a mission hospital in Haiti, to try to eradicate a dreaded mosquito-borne disease. He was looking forward to Christmas for many reasons, one of which was that it coincided with his first anniversary of marriage to his wife Cathy. But all that changed at solstice, on the new road, at the time of least light. Instead, his unclaimed body rotted in the turning, tropical sun.

I did not know Joseph, but a friend from the States who knew his wife called me four days after the killing, to ask me if I could find the body. And so, I had to go up against the gates of hell. I could never describe what was involved in this. His body had already been taken by his killers and dumped in the scrublands, where it was being eaten by animals. And so I had to deal with people who are like rats, like people that have given up their souls, to try to get his body back for his desperate wife, so she could cherish and honor her husband with a Christian burial. Daily phone calls back and forth with her, as I kept trying ... so many obstacles and dangers. Christmas, and their anniversary, drew near. At one point, Cathy said she could not have a better Christmas present that to have the body of her husband brought home. Imagine this! Imagine how desperate life can be. I also became desperate, in wanting to help Cathy in mercy's name. My dealings with these people continued—these killers who stash the bodies of their victims in desolate ravines, stripping them of clothes that might have any value, tunneling their way through these desolate areas of corpses. These were my "dialogue partners." These were the people to whom I had to try to introduce the concept of mercy. They wanted money for the corpse, ransom even for a dead body. And they ripped us off of the part of the ransom we paid.

As I tried through many ways to get Joseph's body, my work with the destitute sick continued. One morning, as I had a prayer with about a hundred people who came to me for help, I prayed for Cathy and for the return of Joseph's body. These people, so sick from tuberculosis and AIDS, asked me about Joseph and Cathy and were heartsick to hear of the tragedy. They asked if I could get a picture of Joseph. They wanted to go into the ravines and look for him themselves. They could not imagine Cathy's suffering. And they would not tolerate it, without trying to help. I made a quick phone call, and asked someone to download Joseph's photo from the university website, and to make 50 copies of it. In a half an hour, I had those pictures. It was the first time I saw the face of the man I was looking for so passionately.

Then, before my eyes, these very sick people formed lines and made plans as to how to cover the ravines. An army of half dead people was heading off to try to right the wrong, the terrible wrong, of a grieving widow and an unburied corpse. You should have seen them, off to do battle against hell itself—thin as rails, struggling to breath, holding themselves on sticks they use for crutches. My eyes watered as I said to God, are these really the only people you have to do battle against hell? Are these really the people? And I heard an answer deep in my heart. "Yes, these ARE the people. They are exactly the people. These blessed, beautiful people." Before the size of their task, they appear to be as small as mustard seeds. But fueled by mercy and compassion, they would spend whatever life was left in them, to move mountains for mercy's sake.

There was a major flaw in our attempt. Fr. Tom, Joseph's best friend, had come to help me. I really needed help to identify the body, if we found it. As I told him, we could find plenty of corpses, especially if we were paying for them. But I would have no idea which was Joseph. The trouble was that we were both too high profile—as Americans and as priests. In law, if there is no body, there is no crime. As long as the body was not produced there was no crime. The killers feared recrimination—not from the peasant posse, but from men like Tom and I, with connections to the American embassy, the Vatican embassy, and the UN—even though we had promised we would not use these. Our mission was pastoral, not political, or legal.

So in the end, we never did recover Joseph's body, but we did our absolute best to do so. And our best was a defiance against hell. Our best used mercy to protest savageness. Our best declared in the face of evil that there is a God-given order to life, and that sacred boundaries must never be violated. Our best showed that mercy has no fear, that love is stronger than death, and there are many people who will give the last ounce of their strength to try to even partially right a wrong.

There were three other incidents, equally as horrible, that marked out the winter months. It would be as hard to me to write about them as it would be for you to read about them. But they all show the same truth: In the face of the arrogant and horrible display of hell, there appears a powerful force of good capable of defying it, and often this goodness is in a seemingly very feeble form. That force of goodness has made its home in you and I.

This is the best of all weeks to meditate on these truths. Holy Week starts today. This is the week when a most brutal death will be delivered to the most noble person ever born. This is the week when Christ will enter into direct conflict with the forces of evil, even descending into hell after being ravaged by it. This is the week when, in the face of evil, the force of goodness will seem very feeble … at least until the end, when it is radiant and eternal. But this is also the week when the sun crosses our threshold again, marking the springtime and the return to life, with a beautiful display of light. This, also, is no coincidence.

We are asked to relive these mysteries during this week. They are as real today as they were two millennia ago. Evil is still evil, but goodness is still so, so good! May God keep mercy and goodness alive in our hearts, and increase our engagement to stand with our brothers and sisters around the world who know the brutal blows of life. But may we all know the blessings and joys of Easter.

Fr. Richard Frechette CP

7

The Deceased Pope and the Risen Christ

April 17, 2005

On this fourth Sunday of the celebration of Christ, risen from the dead, our liturgy speaks strongly of the powerful word of the true shepherd. Not the hireling, not the uncommitted, or even the false shepherd, but the shepherd whose heart is so right that truth rings out in his very words. The sheep know his voice and follow with full trust.

As we hear these readings today, we do so without our own shepherd. Even though the period of official mourning has ended for John Paul II, and we join our prayers with those of Catholics around the world, begging the Holy Spirit to choose for us another great pastor.

We have two great examples today of the power emanating from the voice of the true shepherd. We have the example of our Lord, whose resurrection we still proclaim. His words are so vibrant that after two millennia, one quarter of the world's population claim him as their Lord. No living person has seen him. He has not been seen by a human being for hundreds of generations. Yet His words ring so true, that billions of people call him their Lord. Yes, with different levels of sincerity, and often with divided hearts, but they call themselves Christian and seek to know his voice in their lives, and his Word in their hearts. Yet, everyone makes their own decision during the course of their life as to how deep in the heart one lets his Word enter.

John Paul II, of revered memory, also had a trusted voice. People do not need to agree with you to revere you. When you speak without superficiality, when you believe what you say in the depths of your heart, when your words are consistently in defense of life and dignity, and proclaiming the greatest values in living, your words have power. Look how the death of John Paul II made the whole world pause and ponder. Not another living person on earth could draw such a response by their death. Presidents, kings, queens, and prime ministers were drawn to his plain wooden coffin, set upon the ground.

When you speak from your heart, people are drawn to you. Yes, even if they do not agree with you. The Church of England separated from Catholicism over five centuries ago, over a royal wedding. Until recent years, they remained much like Catholicism in every way, except for belief in the authority of the pope. It is a real quirk of history that after all these centuries of disagreement, on the occasion of another royal wedding, plans had to be postponed, because the highest political authority in England, the highest religious authority in England, and even the royal groom, were all drawn to the funeral of the pope! God certainly loves a colorful story.

Five weeks ago yesterday, while he was in the Gemelli hospital in Rome and entering into his final agony, the pope wrote his 27th and last letter to the priests of the world. It was his custom to write this letter every year, in preparation for Holy Thursday, which is considered the anniversary of the priesthood and the anniversary of the mass. He compared himself to the other sick in the hospital, whose suffering he recognized and sympathized with, and he emphasized to priests that the faithful people have a right to, and a deep need for, true and sincere priests. The priest has the obligation to unite himself with Christ in every way, so that his heart becomes the heart of Christ, with all the power that it brings. His formula was simply stated, and was probably simple because he had used it himself during his own sixty years of priesthood. He invited priests to make all the words of Christ, spoken during the mass, their own words. "This is my body, given up for you. This is my blood, given up for you." Yes, Father, make the commitment courageously to spend yourself completely, to wear yourself out entirely, to the very end, in service to all who need you, to the glory of God's name.

The more the priest takes on the Christ-heart, the more remarkable he becomes, the more he can encourage other people to do the same. The true heart is a beacon. John Paul's true heart, converted to a Christ-heart through years of prayer, beckoned millions to Rome at the time of his death and multimillions around the globe to ponder the meaning of his life and death. And by preferring to be placed in a simple wooden box, unembalmed, placed on the ground and later buried in the earth, he showed that this secret is available to all people, not only to popes or princes.

That we live in extraordinarily troubling times is an understatement. Human life seems to be losing its very humanity, and surrendering itself to violence and money and superficial existence. The consequences of this are seen easily in the global havoc around us. How hungry people are for a true and sincere voice. Just look at how they responded to that of John Paul's. The scriptures tell us that, already in desolation, the world becomes even more desolate, because there are so few who think with their heart. There are so few whose heart is their center, whose heart is the source of their decision and action. We are invited today by the scriptures, and by our shepherd who is resting in the dust, to think with the heart, the very heart of Christ.

I said before we are at the moment sheep without our universal shepherd. We will always need a shepherd, no matter how old we get. We will always need friends, doctors, confessors, and those who lead us when we are weak, or lost, or confused. But the fact that we need a shepherd does not relieve us from also shepherding. We are obliged to shepherd those in need of our friendship, our advice, our Christ light.

For fifty years now, Father Wasson, and all those who join forces with Our Little Brothers and Sisters, have made it a mission to shepherd orphan children. The most lost, the most vulnerable. We seek them in the most difficult countries, in the most trying circumstances. We strive to bring love to them. We go where love is most needed and where it is most difficult to bring it. This is our mission. And even when all our beds are full, when our budgets are strained, when our shepherds are tired beyond words from their many struggles, we still reach out even more. We reach out beyond the boundaries of our own mission: to children living in dumps, to children with terrible disabilities, to children on the streets, to children in prisons, to children be-leaguered by floods, to children in need everywhere.

It is said by ancient holy people that the Passion of Christ started when he was born. It is not limited to his final agony. His whole life was a Passion. At Our Little Brothers and Sisters, our option for the poor, our seeking Christ in his contemporary Passion, is honored by deliberately seeking out the Christ-child in anguish.

At this watershed moment, at this moment of ending and beginning, of death and new life, of continued Easter joy, let us ask God very simply that we all might be blessed with living faith. Let us ask that we might, through prayer, be lead to the Christ-heart. We ask God to make us true, and that our truth ring out in such a way as to produce fruit that will last for all people to the glory of God's name.

Eternal rest grant unto him, O Lord, and let perpetual light shine upon him. And let it be this very light that makes our hearts wise and our lives true.

Fr. Richard Frechette, CP

8

The Children of Cain ... and Other "All Souls" to Be

October 31, 2005

A drop in a bucket doesn't matter too much if the bucket is full (although it does lead to overflowing, which is an image of God's generosity and abundant grace). But a drop in an empty bucket is a good start, and is an image of God's tenacious desire for us to have life, to have it fully, and to have it eternally. God doesn't give up on us.

Consider this prayer, chanted recently over Benedictine monks, good friends of mine, as they lay face down on the floor during their final profession: "O God, source of Holiness, in your great love you created the human family, intending us to share in your divine nature. This loving design of yours was not extinguished by our sins, nor has all the wickedness of the world the power to alter it."

What a powerful thought that is! God's design must be absolutely unshakable, since it holds up against all the wickedness of the word. The world can be pretty wicked place.

The day before yesterday, when we arrived at Wharf Jeremy for our medical clinic, we were met with a gruesome shock. A gang from Cité Soleil had come to the wharf, by canoe in the night, to rob an anchored ship. When they were not able to force entry, or force the ship's staff to open the door, they set the ship on fire after dousing it with gallons of a crude sugar cane rum called clairin. When we arrived, the charred remains of three very young men, whose twisted postures and frightful grimaces showed the agony in which they had died, lay on the wharf, as the market went on as normal. Some women were crying, and there were many gawking unschooled children. (They were getting a very destructive kind of schooling, whereby they are exposed to very bitter realities of life, and then abandoned to their own feelings and conclusions.)

We entered into the fray, appalled and retching, placing their bodies in clean white bags, which always remind me of funeral palls. It brought a bit of dignity and privacy to that inferno, but it also brought hoards of the curious. As the growing crowd peered at me, I invited everyone to prayer. We prayed for the dead and for their families, and we sang a hymn. At the end, an old woman cried out desperately, "We are only animals. Look how we live, and how we die. We are no better than animals."

Yes, it would be easy to think so. In fact, all of the world's wickedness aims to convince us of that. But animals don't en-shroud their dead in clean white garments, or cry for them, or gather together to sing over them. Neither do animals lament the fact that they may be just miserable animals. No, we are not animals. We are people. In wretched situations at times, yes, but we are people- embraced by a huge Godly design. But it is also true that in the face of such overwhelming wretchedness, a simple act of kindness to the living or the dead, is just a drop in the bucket.

Two months ago, I found myself in the challenging position of trying to organize for 1,500 gallons of water a day to be delivered to the infamous Cité Soleil, home of these canoe gangs, and other roving criminals, and kidnappers. It is also home to many honest and dirt-poor peasants for whom, as die-hard missionaries know, food and water are luxuries. In such a place, 1,500 gallons of water is literally only a drop in the bucket. But how many throngs of poor people will line up for this little drop! To make this water reach the poor, I had to meet and talk with the four main gang leaders of the vast slum. These are the people that have of Port-au-Prince terrorized, and who keep the United Nations multinational forces both busy and employed.

The dialogue opened up a whole other world to me, an underworld that is confusing and frightful, but which strangely enough begins to make sense, in the same way that a psychologist can begin to understand what is behind the behavior of a deeply disturbed person. This is not an attempt to accept or justify this underworld, any more than a psychologist accepts or justifies disturbed behavior. But dialogue opens the way to understanding since it reveals worldviews, and worldviews can be challenged by the light of truth, and only this challenging dialogue can make change a possibility.

Our dialogue was fruitful enough to guarantee that the water truck and its drivers would not be harmed, hijacked, or kidnapped. This promise has been respected for these past eight weeks, and continues to be respected. Influence for the good is possible when you can tap into the innate goodness of another person, which may not always be easy or even possible to find.

Even though the deliveries of water have gone well, I was left with a haunting image. When I went to speak to the gangs and found myself in the presence of a bunch of loaded guns, I was disturbed to find that some of the gang members, peering at me from the loaded triggers, were children. I shuddered as I wondered if children are among the canoe raiders. I know they are making themselves felt as a force in society. Just a week before, one of my colleagues was held up and robbed by a group of ragged kids who he thought were stopping his car to beg. Surely there is no future for a country whose children are soldiers or gangsters, who burn and rob and kill. Unless.....

Unless what?

Unless, as the prophet Isaiah said, their "swords are beaten into plowshares, and the spears into pruning hooks." This prophecy is very much needed in our world. The phenomenon of the child soldier, or the child gangster, is ever too real around the globe. I recently saw a bullet that was cut lengthwise and then shaped into a cross. The base of the bullet was the stand that held the cross upright. It was made by a child soldier in Africa, after a priest showed him that this was also a good use for a bullet: fashioning it into an object of religious art. It is probably even the best use of a bullet. This bullet-cross really struck me, as I held it in my hands and examined it. It challenged me to think hard. Why not turn a bullet into education? Why not start a few small schools for these children, the only tuition being a gun? And why not burn the tuition at the door, after dousing it with crude clairin, on the first day of school? Why not? How many schools burn their tuition on the first day of school, to teach everyone a lesson? Odd measures, but after all, these are very odd times.

Obviously, there would be no way of pulling this new idea off, without another trip to the gang leaders, and getting their help. But I would start with just one this time: Belony, who replaced the murdered Dread Wilmer. Dread was killed by one of his own, for thirty pieces of silver (actually for more like $15,000). But this present-day Judas also met an end so bad I wouldn't even describe it to you here. His name was "Tou Mouri," which means "Also Dead." He could not have been better named.

The atrocity of the boat burning made me doubt that I could succeed with this idea, of starting a small trade school for the child gangsters to get them out of violence. How could I, in conscience, continue to dialogue with men who would order such an abomination? I was thinking about this for a good while, when the news reached me that the eleven young men who had burned the boat were savagely killed in Cité Soleil. It seems that even hell finds some crimes reprehensible. At least this showed me the crime was not ordered by the gang leaders. This does not make the gang leaders saints. It does mean that, at least for me, dialogue is still possible. Not because of the revenge, but because they were not part of the crime.

In death, I saw once again very dramatically how darkness surges to swallow up those who serve it, both in the case of Tou Mouri, and these eleven young arson-murderers. But I have also seen many times how, as it says in the book of Wisdom, the whole universe lines up behind the ones trying to do right, and aligns its strength to make the good purpose flourish.

Belony explained to me that probably some 250 children in his "dominion" had weapons. Most had machetes, knives, or zam kreol (which are homemade guns). Only some have large guns. He explained that most of the kids who have weapons took them up for a simple reason. They had seen their mothers or fathers killed by violence. Imitation is still the best teacher. Now we need to get these children to imitate something else ... something full of life, full of tomorrow.

Meetings with the other three leaders were also encouraging, and gave a small glimmer of hope that this mission might be possible. Now, to work out the details with them, and Fr. Guiton, who is practically the last priest left in Cité Soleil. Fr. Guiton will collaborate with us and loan us his school building for the purpose. He is young, brave, hardworking, and dedicated. He feels very strongly that this will be a necessary witness to peace, to options other than violence. But he also knows, as do I, that this is just a drop on the bucket.

But a drop in a bucket makes for a good start. It's about as big as a bullet, and its dull thud is a little bit like a shot- the shot to signal the run to freedom.

Fr. Richard Frechette, CP

9

Jonah under the Withered Tree

January 24, 2006

Yesterday, I sat on a hot rock on a hot road in the hot sun in a hot slum, for nearly an hour, trying to get my senses back. I don't remember ever being so sad and tired, so sick of it all, so overcome with feelings of hopelessness and futility. That the rock was in the middle of the infamous Cité Soleil is not exactly a sideline to the story. If anyone thinks Cité Soleil is a tropical paradise, today's *New York Times* would have set them straight. Even the UN is afraid to go there, as are the two million inhabitants of Port-au-Prince. I was there to answer a simple question: Can you or can't you trust in the basic goodness of human beings? I had always believed you could, but now I was absolutely in doubt. And it wasn't just a red truck, but even my vocation, that hung in the balance.

It all started on Sunday, when we were bitten by the ancient serpent of evil—and it was a very nasty bite. Our whole funeral team, which mercifully buries destitute dead almost daily, was kidnapped from the cemetery at Drouillard, as they set out to bury a small child who died in our hospital. Yes, the whole group, even the small dead body—gone in a minute with a band of thugs.

Then they were separated by the thieves. The grieving mother was pulled violently from the red truck that serves as our hearse. She was robbed, harassed, threatened and then told to run for her life, bullets ringing out after her. Frantically she ran, terrorized, not even knowing where to go—and having no idea if and where her precious child would be laid to rest. Mario was hauled back up to the cemetery where he was robbed of the few dollars he had. He was threatened with death, reproached strongly for having so little money and his pocket, and sent running for his life, as had been the mother.

Fred and the dead child were taken in the red truck, deep into the slums at Drouillard. It seems that someone from the gang suddenly saw things by a human light, and said to their leader, "Boss, he was going to bury this child. Why don't you let him go and just keep the truck?" Fred found himself dismissed with a grunt, and, after being robbed, went walking the few kilometers back to the cemetery in the hot sun, with the coffin balanced on his head, heavy with its precious load. This road was absolutely deserted, and he had every reason to fear an attack from any quarter. But, as we all know, the worse attacks for anyone always come from within.

Somewhere along that abandoned roadway, as he made his way so carefully, the serpent bit again. Fred himself had grown up in our orphanage, and his past life included some time in prison. Because of his own self-doubt, which haunted him even though he had become a very hardworking and productive member of our team, he suddenly found himself thinking that I would never believe that he was kidnapped, and the red truck stolen. Surely, I would see that story as a cover-up for him stealing the truck himself. Tormented by these thoughts, which grew in strength in the course of the long hot day, his mind became more twisted and distorted. So much so, that when I finally met him for the first time since his ordeal, he launched a full-scale verbal rage at me, accusing me of caring nothing for his situation and doing nothing to help.

I was absolutely baffled, and had no idea what he was thinking. In fact, as soon as I had gotten the call that he was kidnapped (as I was starting Sunday mass at our orphanage in the mountains) by cell phone I had already organized an army of people to help him. And I was assured by the gang leaders that he would be released. But none of this would matter to him in his tormented state of mind. Now it was my turn to be doubly stung.

I am not a stranger to Cité Soleil. We have many mission activities there: water delivery, schools, clinics, emergency medical help, ice cream runs for the children, etc. I had no hesitation heading there to get to the bottom of this whole incident with the gangs. As soon as I arrived, I chose that hot rock in the middle of the street as the throne of my protest. Two different gang leaders came to talk to me, Bazou and Evans. Why was I on the rock? If I wanted the truck back why didn't I just say so? Please go home, we will send the truck to you before the end of the day. OK, so you refuse to go without the truck. At least move to the shade until we get it. We will buy you a Coke.

It wasn't just the truck. I was protesting what was done to a dead child, to a grieving mother, to Fred and Mario, to my whole team, to the whole country, to my faith. The LAST thing it was about was a truck.

When I wouldn't budge, Bazou finally said to me, "Mon Pere, have you gone crazy?"

Am I crazy? Are you sure your question is for me? Your friends kidnap the dead, and I am the crazy one? Why are you crushing the people? Your own people? A very poor people with hard lives? Why? This poor women, already weighed down by poverty and sorrow and grief, had this small chance to bury her child with tenderness. And you terrorized an already defeated woman. If we didn't bury this child ourselves, the body would wind up at Ti Tanyin as food for dogs and pigs. On top of her poverty and sadness you heaped on terror, and send her running in fear and despair. And you have the audacity to ask me if I am crazy?

The red truck was rolled up to me, curbside. Complete: battery and jack, radio and papers. "Here now. Please get out of the sun. They didn't know it was one of your trucks. Why don't you mark all your trucks a certain way so everyone will know them?"

Really? Do we need to mark even a coffin? Are even the dead not spared this nightmare?

When I finally got home, I stopped in the chapel for a quiet minute. There in the corner was Fred, sobbing. I sat next to him and he flooded with tears. He had heard that I went myself to Cité Soleil for the truck. So he knew I would believe his story. He let out his doubt, that I would never have believed him. Deep sobs. "Fred, you are keeping yourself in your own prison now. This kind of thinking will never help you. It's no good for you. I am your friend and I believe in you. That's what's good for you. And you are good for me. For God's sake, you need to be careful not to fall into this twisted thinking."

I took off the simple cross I have worn around by neck for many years and placed it around his neck. No great gift as far as jewelry goes, but I needed to give him a deep sign of solidarity, something to stay with him.

Then he asked me if I knew what was the worse part of the whole ordeal, for himself. He explained to me that the worse part was standing helplessly as the poor grieving mother ran off in confusion and anguish. How he wished he could find her and help her, and tell her that he saw the funeral all the way to the end, and had buried her small son tenderly. As I watched his swollen eyes and heard to his pained words, all my faith and force returned to me with a surge.

Anyway, off to bed. This is more than enough for one day. But not without singing for evening prayer a favorite hymn:

"We will run, and not grow weary, for our God will be our strength,
And we will fly like the eagle, we will rise again."

Fr. Rick Frechette, CP

10

The Presentation of the Lord …
and the Art of Un-Kidnapping
(A Celebration of Light)

February 2, 2006

Nearly a week ago, we were working in a tiny shack, dark and hot, doing our best to take care of very sick poor people in Cité Soleil. It is not easy, trying to make the most of the few scattered stands of light, available through the bullet holes in the tin roof. Out on the street, I suddenly saw a crowd of children, a whole lot of them, walking and giggling. What a nice sound it was! I went out for a breath of air, and to see what they were doing. In the middle of the throng were two veiled heads. Two nuns from Spain, who work in this shell-shocked slum, were walking along and talking to these many children as they went to visit the sick. I went to say hello to them. Sister Marta raised her head and looked at me with her piercing green eyes. "We have to pray hard, mon pere. We live now in total darkness." I said, "Yes, Sister. But you are giving a beautiful light to these children, and they are shining with their own little flames."

The light that comes from Christ is always beautiful and always new, and graces any setting—even the tragic settings of absolute poverty.

Two prophets mark today's feast—Simeon and Ann. Ann's prophecies are not in recorded memory, but Simeon speaks of the light of Christ, a light for the nations, which will give long awaited peace. This is the Christ who came to ransom us while we were still slaves, to lead us from the prison of darkness into the freedom of the children of light. I had never before considered that the whole Christian religion is centered around the idea of ransom—a price paid by Christ our Light to set us free from darkness. Yes, a price was paid for our freedom, for our salvation. St. Paul says outright that we were bought, with the price of Christ's blood. This is a brilliant and vibrant image, when you find yourself pricing and buying back captive people, when applying all you forces and skills to set them free from the hands that imprison them.

My team and I have not gone into this challenge by choice, this "ministry of un-kidnapping." But we are in it—at least sometimes. In fact, as soon as I would finish seeing the sick people filling these nooks and crannies, for the seventeenth time in very few months our task would be to try to liberate someone else from the sinister industry of trafficking in human beings. The fact that this time it was an 85-year-old French nun (and her three companions) made swift success all the more urgent. They had already been captive for a few days.

I recently visited a highly controversial Haitian priest in prison. He is sick with leukemia, and we spoke of many things, including his own circumstances and illness. I learned that the major criminal charge against him is "association with evildoers." It made me pause. My team and I also associate with "evildoers," all the time. But, obviously, never to help them do evil. To the contrary, we try to influence them to do good. These "evildoers" were once again the very people that I needed—to free the elderly Sister.

As was the case once again, I did not know the people we were trying to free. Once it was a young missionary priest from Czech Republic named Roman. Another time, a young businessman from India named Jerome. Now there was Sister Agnes and her companions from France. But I did not know them. They were just names. Each time, I had been asked by a consulate, a chancery, or by a grieving brother or friend, to use my association with "evildoers" to try to do something good. I have never been called by kidnappers themselves who, announcing their catch, then ask what we will pay. In fact, the kidnappers always lose money when I get involved. So do I.

A few times we did not pay any ransom. I was enough of a wordsmith, and there were enough angels around, to wedge open the door to freedom. Sometimes I have paid very little—in fact a pittance. "We would like to give them to you for free, mon pere. We won't charge for our part. But we still have to pay the ones who caught them, the ones who delivered them, the one whose house they are staying in, the one who makes them food, the one who makes sure they don't get away." It is easy to see that this is a whole industry, a perverted hotel industry involving captured guests.

Sometimes I have paid bigger money, but still not so big. And I mean nowhere near the asking price. I settled early on a philosophy. Christ did not ask that the price he paid to free us be returned to him. Nor would I. My involvements in setting captives free would be a dead loss; a lifesaving dead loss.

But I am also smart politically. If I don't accept any money for the ransom I have paid, when a ransom of some sort is necessary, I can never be accused by either side of having made a profit in these dealings. And hopefully, I will never be a priest in a Haitian prison with the charge "kidnapping, and association with evildoers."

But to be truthful, setting the unknown captive free is delicate work. It's not just about paying. That's the easiest part. Finding them is a challenge. The negotiation is full of red flags. You run the danger of being distrusted from all sides. The interpretation by others of your involvement is far from benign. You find yourself in violent areas, sometimes in the night, sometimes with a good bit of money in your pocket. It's all part of it. But then the captives are brought to you, their feet shuffling and stumbling along in the dark, your truck ready to take them swiftly to the freedom and protection for their embassy. You hear them shuffling along dark alleyways toward you. Then they are safe in your truck, and they are free.

And many times at the moment of their release, there is another manifestation of light. I remember Fr. Roman spoke mostly of how moved he was by the poverty of his captors, and a great pity for what their lives are like. The light of compassion shone brightly in him. Jerome spoke of some bonds of closeness with others who were held with him. The light of solidarity shone brightly in him. But Sister Agnes! Now there is a high-spirited woman! As I helped this 85-year-old nun into the truck to whisk her off to the French embassy, she said to me, "At my age, about the only thing missing from my curriculum vitae was being kidnapped!" The light of humor shone brightly in her. These lights rend Satan and his legions completely impotent. Because of these lights, the ordeal of these people cannot ravage their souls.

There are other lights as well. All the kidnapper extras, who "hosted" her, walked Sister to the truck. The warm embraces were mutual. It was as if they were seeing their grandmother off. One even said, "I hope you come again!" What a strange world.

It is a dirty business, kidnapping. But it is done by human beings, all of whom, like us, alternate in allegiance to light and to darkness. God said, "I set before you light and darkness, life and death. Choose life." I have always believed that people's choices can be altered with the right influence, if they see by the right kind of light. Sometime you and I can be that light.

I know that paying ransom perpetuates this dirty business. But do you leave a grandmother in chains to make a point? Did Christ decide against freeing us when He knew that, even after paying the highest price, we would be taken by sin over and over and over again?

It is important to analyze the causes of kidnapping. It was once expressed as a political payback: you kidnapped our president, now we will kidnap you. But now it is a high-yield business in a country of massive unemployment where most people live on less than a dollar a day. Until the causes are addressed, the debates on whether or not to pay ransom will always be predictable: It will be easy to hold the opinion ransom should never be paid, until someone you love is suddenly gone.

Christ our light, help us to see clearly. Christ our light, help us to decide rightly. Lighten the dark and tangled ways that make up our life's journey.

Give us hearts eager to be led by the kindly light of love, and the peace prophesied by your servant Simeon.

Fr. Richard Frechette CP

11

Good Fridays, Bad Choices— Voodoo and the Passion of Christ

Easter Monday
April 17, 2006

"You can't answer the cell phone during prayers," I said to myself. "Especially during these prayers at the hour that Christ died."

"But this is probably an emergency, and you are a doctor as well as a priest!"

"No, it's not right. Don't answer it."

Whenever I talk to myself, the dialogue is always feisty.

The phone buzzed in my pocket, unanswered, three persistent times. It could wait. The prayers would be over in just a few more minutes. The phone buzzed again. I discreetly looked at it, just to see what name appeared on the screen. It was Raphael. That could mean only one thing: that she was dead.

My blood turned cold, and a shiver ran down my spine. The houngan (voodoo priest) had told this perfectly healthy young woman, just a week ago, that she would not live past the "prayers of Calvary hill." It was in her cards. She could not live past the hour of Christ's death, unless she drank the potion he could make to save her. Now sure enough, she was dead. As the prayers of Calvary hill were coming to their conclusion, so was she coming to hers.

Her name was Marie Louise. She and her brothers and sisters were born to impoverished Haitian cane cutters in the bitter sugar fields of the Dominican Republic. The mother and father died, and the children were thrown over the border into Haiti a dozen years ago, during one of the frequent Haitian roundups by Dominican officials. They landed in Haiti where they had never lived, where they knew no one, and where they could not even speak the local Creole language. A woman who saw them had pity on them and gathered them up, delivering them to our orphanage, where we have spent many years getting to know and love, and struggling to deal with, this complex family.

Earlier Good Friday morning, while enjoying a coffee, a few of us were getting ready to start the day. I was on my way to visit a friend who has his own cross to bear, in the form of brain cancer. Good Friday was a good day for such a visit, since on this day we commemorating the strength of grace in an absolutely stark reality. A grace as dark as it was powerful. Our chatter was interrupted by a disturbing call. Marie Louise was very sick in Kenscoff, and needed help. Off we went. Sure enough, her condition was disastrous. It was clear to me immediately that her whole nervous system was under full-scale attack. I was sure she was reeling from a poison. We did our best to resuscitate and stabilize her, and when there was nothing more we could add to her treatments, I left her in the care of Raphael. I had other sick people to see, and I also needed to be on time for the prayers at 3 pm at the orphanage on the mountain. I thought Marie Louise stood a small chance with our treatments. I had seen these things before. Usually there is a lot of hysteria associated with them.

I underestimated this time how much was terror and how much was poison. I didn't underestimate in terms of treatment, but in terms of hope. I did not expect her to die.

In shock, I uttered the final "prayer of Calvary hill." I had no idea what to think or what to do next. But for sure, I needed to get her body. The Sisters and children of the orphanage started to pray the rosary for Marie Louise. Alfonso and I headed to Port-au-Prince to find a coffin, and to bring her body home.

It was a long sad drive back up the mountain. It was late at night, and we gathered to bath her body and dress her, and place her in the coffin. As we bathed her, I thought of Joseph of Aramathea, and the sacred body he prepared for burial, freshly taken off the cross, two millennia ago that very day. Both his corpse and ours were destroyed by jealousy and hatred. And there was no lack of blood in either case. His, from many afflicted wounds, hers from massive internal bleeding that poured out her mouth and nose as we prepared her for burial. Across the span of twenty centuries, we understood the sadness and the urgency of what Joseph had done for the dead Christ- the last possible act of kindness and respect.

Joseph had to observe the Jewish command to bury Jesus before sunset. We were supposed to observe the Catholic command not to bury Marie Louise until after these high Holy Days. But we could not keep her unembalmed body, in the tropics, and full of poisons, in an orphanage, until Monday. We had no choice but to arrange a simple burial, with prayers and without a funeral mass, on Holy Saturday morning.

Timid heads of hundreds of orphan children peered into her coffin. Alfonso, with wet eyes and trembling hands, placed an image of the risen Christ into her cold hands. Susana and others who spoke a last goodbye did so with quivering and broken voices. And all of us had hearts as heavy as lead.

We struggled to understand the story, the one that Marie Louise had herself painted. She had come to see Alfonso a week before, to explain a grave problem. She was in love with a man who already had a girlfriend and a child. She also had become pregnant by him. Even though the boyfriend tragically insisted on her ending the pregnancy a few months earlier, there was still strong jealousy on the part of the other woman, who went to see a houngan to put a death curse on her. A different houngan, whom she sought for help, wanted $300 Haitian dollars to make a potion to protect her. Marie Louise was looking for that money.

Alfonso insisted, rightly, that God's power is absolute, that to buy into these cures and this way of thinking is like stepping into quicksand. To stay close to the God of life, and to stay away from these evil incantations and their hypnotic power, was the only way to face them. (Good Friday is the most dramatic expression of this message imaginable.) He gave Marie Louise a cross to wear around her neck, to remind her of God's love and power. Such discussions are almost daily occurrences in Haiti, so alive are the convictions that misfortune, illness, and death are caused by bad magic.

Two days before her fateful one, Marie Louis was at the orphanage again. A lovely dress, fresh makeup, cheerful conversation, helping in the kitchen. But before she left, she asked again for $300, which was once again denied.

Desolation of desolations. After her burial, we went to Kenscoff to try to understand more fully everything that had happened. I spoke with the boyfriend, the two girls who lived with her, with neighbors. I tried to find the houngan. I spent Easter Sunday in this dreary pursuit, only to find out that Marie Louise's life was one of prostitution and drugs, of nightlong parties in filthy bars. Desolation of desolations. Those who filled her days and nights were nowhere to be found when she needed them. We were the only ones to try to rescue her from deadly poisons, to shed tears for her, to prepare her tenderly for burial, to commend her to the earth with prayers for her soul. Desolation of desolations. In spite of all her years with us, she never centered herself in what is true about love, but sought it in the places where, as the Bible says, Satan crouches like a lion ready to devour you if you are foolish enough to go near. Desolation of desolations. Marie Louise had come to us as child out of a nightmare, only to leave us as a young woman into a nightmare again. But this I know for sure: at five years old and again at twenty years old, we were truly home and family for her. May she rest in that comfort now.

Religions have always played contradictory roles in society. Some aspects are liberating and life-giving. Others are enslaving and destructive. Christianity has dealt some deathblows in her long and very human history. So has Voodoo. But Christianity is a religion that lives in the public eye, with identifiable authorities that must take responsibility for her activity in society. Voodoo lives in the shadows, ever secretive, with never anyone to hold responsible. Christianity must continually restate her purpose and goals, ever refined by public challenge. Superstitions become replaced by convincing descriptions of mystery, and the demands of mystery on us. Maybe one day Voodoo will be forced into this essential dynamic.

Late that night, Good Friday, after a long tragic day, I stepped outside exactly at midnight to look at the stars. There was a wonder in the sky. The Southern Cross, of all things, shone like a diamond in the velvet sky, beneath clouds lit up by the full Easter moon. I thought of God's promise to Noah after the great flood. It was a promise of life, sealed by the sign of the rainbow. If there could ever be a rainbow at midnight, there it was, before me in the dark sky.

"Desperado, won't you come down from you fences,
Put down your defenses, and open the gate.
It may be raining, but there's a rainbow above you.
You better let somebody love you
Before its too late."*

*Don Henley and G. Frey

Fr. Richard Frechette, CP

12

To Eulogize a Saint:
The Life and Death of
Fr. William Bryce Wasson

Founder: Nuestros Pequeños Hermanos International
August 26, 2006

When I was a young priest, I remember very well when I met Fr. Bill Wasson for the first time. With a soft and sincere voice, brimming with enthusiasm, he spoke of the multitudes of orphaned children under his care in Mexico. While he spoke to me, I experienced something that is hard to describe and that I had never felt before. Invisible ropes started to surround and bind me, "cords of commitment," and then I felt myself being pulled in a direction that I had not intended go, indeed a direction that I even resisted.

Fr. Bill persisted. He told me that if I would come to help the mission of the Pequeños Hermanos, I must be prepared for trials. I would have a million problems. But he promised: if I kept faith, and worked and prayed hard, I would also find a million solutions. How interesting and challenging this sounded. And I thought to myself, "What a nice and wise man."

Little did I realize that it was Fr. Bill himself who would lead me, head-on, into all those problems! This was Fr. Bill's way. If he felt you were up for a challenge, he would lure you into deep waters. Once you were over your head, you were forced to swim hard, to work hard, to pray hard, to dream hard, to analyze hard, and to depend on God and other people. And in the end you found yourself speaking new languages, knowing many cultures and peoples, adept in skills you had never learned or thought you would need—in a word you find you have become richer and stronger in mind, heart and soul.

In the Catholic mass in honor of a saint, the preface confidently states: "in every generation God raises up men and women outstanding in holiness." Let's get this straight. We are not talking about plastic or artificial people. If anything, the Bible, which is the best mirror of humanity, shows us that God works with who we are, faults and flaws, and makes our humanity the cornerstone of His activity among us. God uses us as we are, because God loves colorful and human stories. And if we want, if we agree to let God have a great influence in our soul, our own stories become God-stories. The life of Fr. Bill has become yet one more colorful and wondrous God-story, and has given astounding and lasting fruit.

This only happens, by the way, if we agree to let God intertwine His life with ours. We have to agree. And we are free not to! Grace builds on nature, but only if we say "yes." Here is an example of grace building on nature. Fr. Bill comes from this land, from this city of Phoenix. The Phoenix is an ancient mythical bird that dies in flames and ashes and rises again in three days. You can see why the Phoenix is a natural early Christian symbol of the resurrection of Christ. When Fr. Bill was a child, Phoenix was a cattle town of hot sand. It is hard for life to thrive in a desert. Over these years Phoenix has become a vast and abundantly alive city. When you come from Phoenix, resurrection is in your bones.

But when you have faith, you take this even further, as did Fr. Bill. Let's think about it. When we are born we have a human destiny. We will live, work, have a family, strive to be happy. When we are baptized we are given a mission. We call it a vocation. Our mission is to find the best way to fulfill our human destiny, and at the same time to build the city of God. Fr. Bill was baptized into his mission in this church of St. Mary. He served mass at this high altar for many years as a young boy. Try to imagine back 75 years. Picture little Billy Wasson standing right here, holding huge and heavy books full of Latin for the priest to read. From here, at this altar, until his death a week ago, the mass was always precious to Fr. Bill. He studied in school here, right behind this Church, and heard his priestly calling here, in this place. And what was the mission given to him?

To be the Phoenix, the sign and the agent of resurrection, for children everywhere whose lives had become ashes, whose bodies and hearts and minds had become scorched like desert sand by poverty, tragedy, sickness and war. This was his mission, and it burned itself into him and gave him a lifelong and single-minded goal and focus, and the mission had such an urgency to it, it made it almost impossible for Fr. Bill to ever rest.

But let's not forget, Fr. Bill's way of achieving this mission was as a priest. "Priest" means "the one who offers sacrifice for the people." But the best priest is the one whose life IS a sacrifice for the people. Fr. Bill sacrificed himself, as a priest and as a person, for the mission of Nuestros Pequeños Hermanos commended to him by God. He spent himself, to the very end, on this. He worked tirelessly when he was healthy and when he was sick. When he was happy and when he was depressed, he continued working after a long fight with cancer, after losing his spleen, after breaking one hip and then the other, and when age and sickness were as heavy as lead upon him. And what was this work? In the same way that the city of Phoenix was resurrected by the building of many canals bringing lifegiving water, Fr. Bill's life's work was building canals from many lands to the children of Nuestros Pequeños Hermanos, and by building canals between and among the children and staff of Nuestros Pequeños Hermanos. These canals did not bring water, they brought love. Not cheap and sentimental love, but the gospel love called "agape," which is as strong as steel, and is bought only with sacrifice. This is the water of true and everlasting life. For 53 years Fr. Bill, and many friends and colleagues, have built vast networks of canals that give poor and orphan children a chance in life. It is true these canals also bring money and professional services and volunteers, but even these, if they are not underscored by gospel love, are, as St. Paul's says, the clanging of empty bells, and they contribute nothing to building the city of God.

So today we offer this mass, a simple and timeless prayer, a sacrifice, for our brother, Fr. Bill, through whom God has done extraordinary things. And we wish for him the Franciscan blessing that was always on his lips: Paz y Bien (Peace and Well-being) forever.

And for ourselves, I say simply that it is not for nothing that I have tried to show the faith dimension of Fr. Bill's life and work. It is his living faith that has made Nuestros Pequeños Hermanos a vibrant mission that has always enjoyed God's blessing. May God console us in our sorrow, deepen our faith, and fill us with this same gospel love, this same willingness to sacrifice, so that God can do great things through us, and make Nuestros Pequeños Hermanos continue to grow and thrive for children who still wander lost in ashes.

Fr. Rick Frechette, CP

13

Keeping Sabbath

(A Summer Chronicle)
September 11, 2006

When June rolled around a few months ago, was I ever
ready for it. I was so eager to have the saddle off my back for
a while. I was absolutely going to drive my schedule down.
June brought the feeling of old school days: waiting for the
last bell to ring with its promise of three months of rest and
fun. The promise was so real this year I could smell it. It
was in the fresh coffee I would sip as I watched sunrise each
morning, and in the scent of the red hibiscus lining the lane
behind our hospital, where I would take a leisurely walk at
first light. The months go fast, the years even faster. Years
ago, it would soon be time to answer the school bell again,
with an essay, "What I did on my summer's vacation." At
least for me, this was not a vacation but a string of Sabbaths.
Not the "leave your bull in the pit until Monday" kind of
Sabbath, but the kind where you help the paralytic pick up
the mat and walk. My essay would be, "How I did my best
to keep summer Sabbath."

We had enjoyed four months of relative calm in Haiti, from February to June. The election of a president had given a respite of hope. Ironically, in this period of calm and free from daily emergencies, we had our attention drawn again, shockingly, to the depth of the poverty that surrounds us. You don't notice it so much when you are constantly running from bullets and toward emergencies. Summertime would have a lot of difficult challenges in store for us, and would jolt us away from our poverty stare- and summer certainly had no idea of allowing us to rest.

The Feast of Mary Magdalene

June saw a return of violence and kidnapping. It was time once again to be aware of red zones, to be hypervigilant when on the streets, to have at least one companion when on the road. Still with all of this, they tried to kidnap our medical director right off our hospital doorstep at high noon. And when they didn't manage to get her, they set her car on fire.

One day, kidnappers took the whole airport road by storm. The chaos and frenzy had cars jumping curbsides, truck drivers jumping out of moving trucks, cars driving on the wrong side of the street and flipped upside down. The shooting was with heavy artillery. I know—I was there. We were helping the wounded. A number of people died and a lot of people were kidnapped. There were two events that burned themselves into my memory that day, aside from the shock of seeing the airport road look like a car junkyard. There was a family of three kidnapped, in front of the long-closed "Red Planet Market." The father fought with the kidnappers, and was shot dead in front of his wife and young daughter and was lying in the road. The wife and daughter, numb with shock, were kidnapped. When Ti Blanc, the local "boss," heard what had happened, he brought the mother and child out of kidnapping and to the main road where they could get away.

Then we had a phone call from some friends deeper inside the slum. There were two gunshot people badly hurt, but no one could reach them for the gunfire. I drove our truck near the entrance to the area, but it was obvious we could not go in. There was too much shooting. So I thought we would sit and wait and think of what to do. Maybe they would bring the wounded to us in wheelbarrows. Suddenly, a truck full of heavily armed men, all in black, drove up to the intersection from inside the slum. They shot heavy artillery into the air. They were dressed like the special police force, but it was easy to see they were frauds. How? Because the special police eat well, and are strong from bodybuilding. These men were so thin; their clothes were hanging off of them. They were "chimeres" (ghosts) from the slums. I thought the were waging yet another attack, but Raphael understood at once that they were clearing the way for us to go in to get the wounded, which we did. I had never seen the like. We stabilized the wounded and raced them to town, to the surgeons of Doctors Without Borders.

The Seventeenth Sunday of Ordinary Time:
Loaves and Fishes Multiplied

As usual, I started getting calls from people who had friends or family disappear into the hands of kidnappers. I wrote their names, their car license plate numbers, on small scraps of paper, and then made calls to people who scour the slums for a trace of them.

One was a missionary priest from El Salvador. One was a driver for an organization that provides food for poor children, called BND (Bureau of Nutrition and Development). I was able to find them but it was nearly impossible for me to get them free. I was doing my best but getting nowhere. For one thing, the gangs were getting tired of me making them lose money. Also, they were more arrogant now than they were four months ago. Before Preval became president, they were insecure with the interim government that opposed them. Also, at that time, the UN was a higher authority than the non-elected interim government, and the gangs were a bit more leery of them. Now, "their man" Preval was president, and as the legitimately elected leader, he had the upper hand over the UN. The gangs were arrogant and cocky. I decided to give up.

The next morning a few of us were talking and lamenting these changes that had weakened our hand in the slums. And, of course, the phone calls continued. We decided we could not give up. We even had the idea of borrowing a UN army tank and driving it ourselves to the kidnapped holding place and freeing the people. (I can still see the look of absolute disbelief on the face of the bishop when I suggested this idea to him.) In the end, I decided to go back to Cité Soleil with Nebez, the leader of our whole enormous St. Luke Mission, and stay there until we got them out.

We were there until eleven o'clock at night, through blackouts and thunderstorms. We were able to force the hand of the kidnappers for the liberation of Fr. Cesar. I was brought to a dark alley to identify him before we brokered for his exchange. It was dark and he was far off, and I don't see at a distance well without my glasses, which I did not have with me. So I wanted to get out and walk to his car to identify him, but I was not allowed. (Maybe they were afraid if it was not Fr. Cesar, I would also want to free whoever it was!) When I protested that I could not see him, the kidnappers disappeared for a while and came back with a dozen pair of eyeglasses. (They had taken the glasses from everyone in the kidnapped holding place who wore them, and had me try them on, one after another, until I could see well enough to identify Fr. Cesar.)

Then the price of is freedom was mentioned.

What price? I don't pay anything!

There was bickering. They explained they had to pay the one who did the kidnapping, the motorcyclist who brought them at gunpoint into the slum, the owner of the house where they were holed up, the one who made them food everyday, the ones who made sure they didn't run away, etc. This was a business.

No way would I pay! ... at least not what they were asking.

I went back to see one of the gang leaders I know in Cité Soleil, and asked him to call that other gang and badger them down, which he did. It did not make him popular with the other gang. It did not make me popular with either gang. But finally a modest sum was accepted. But then I had another problem. I did not have that money, nor could I get it at that late hour. So I asked the gang to loan me the money (which they did). I also asked them to come with me to get the priest (which they did), since it was very late and that other gang was surely angry with me. And while I was at it, I told them I was nearly out of gas and asked them to fill my tank (which they did). So I was in the unusual situation of having a gang fill my tank, drive me to free Fr. Cesar, and pay the ransom! And that was how we were able to liberate Fr. Cesar and the seminarian who was kidnapped with him. (By the way, they had offered to give me the seminarian earlier, during the eyeglass incident, as a gesture of good faith. To my great admiration, the seminarian refused his freedom if Fr. Cesar was not also being released.)

Fr. Cesar was very disturbed, even shocked, as I lead him out of Cité Soleil and on the road of his freedom. I remember saying to him, "I know this was tough and scary for you, Father.

It is an ugly business. It will take a good while for you to heal inside. But, in a way, life is very much like this in one way or another: some people try to enslave and degrade you, and others try to lift you up and set you free. You are free by the grace of God. You have to make the best use of your freedom and not be pulled into a hole of cynicism and fear."

I went back again into the dark slums, kerosene lamps lining the alleys, for the driver of the food program. He was easy to get at this point. The gangs wanted me out. It was late and they had also had it for one day. I was able to leave with him. But I had to go back the next day to get his car.

Within three days, the director of the food program contacted me. He and the BND organization wanted to help the poor children in our St. Luke programs and schools. Suddenly, we had 2,500 meals a day for our summer programs, and a guarantee of 1,600 meals a day for our schools for the new school year; and the promise of a water truck so we could resume water deliveries to the poor of Cité Soleil. We were astounded at how misfortune had produced food for so many hungry children. It's an ill wind that doesn't blow some good.

The Feast of the Transfiguration

The summer was marked by frequent phone calls and travel, related to the sickness and death of the founder of our works for children in Haiti, Fr. Bill Wasson. He was the founder not only of our "Nos Petits Freres et Soeurs" programs in Haiti, but of those in eight other countries. For 54 years he had worked tirelessly to establish homes for orphaned and abandoned children. As he diminished and weakened with age and sickness, he was given special graces evident to us all. Lifelong restlessness and an urgency to fulfill his mission gave way to peace. He was very patient with his sufferings, which were enormous. (He was not able to eat anything or take a sip of water for the last two months of his life, and could not walk at all—in fact, he could hardly move.) He was not afraid to die, but put himself confidently in God's hands. God gave him time to prepare for death. Many visits with cherished friends, short but strong conversations, occasional Mass at the bedside, followed occasionally by sing-a-longs and jokes—these events marked his final days. And always there was a blessing given.

For us it was also not easy. It was clear we were losing a longtime friend and a strong spirit and force for our life and work. We were trying to apply his "living will" to the delicate and changing issues of his health. It was clear to us immediately that the "living will" (advanced directive as to what to do in case of devastating illness) is not a blueprint but a guide, as constant interpretation was necessary. It was very much a dynamic involvement that was not without agony. But in the end, Fr. Bill died a holy death: he was ready, he was reconciled, he was not afraid, he trusted in God, he was patient, he was kind, he gave blessings. His whole life had prepared him for his moment, when he was, as St. Paul says, transformed at the twinkling of an eye, and given a body of light.

The Feast of the Assumption

The unbelievable had happened. Sister Abha was shot. This was really surpassing all limits—that one of Mother Teresa's sisters would be shot. How could they do this? The Sisters live with the poor, they live poorly themselves, they care for the poorest of the poor. Especially Sister Abha, who opened their mission in Haiti, with Mother Teresa herself, 28 years ago. She has worked tirelessness in Haiti for all these years. To add salt to the wound, the shooting was ordered and paid for by a young man she had taken off the streets and raised from the time he was a small child. Fortunately she had pushed the arm of the thief as he fired his gun, and the bullet pulverized one of the bones of her forearm rather than piercing her chest. We were able to get her to Florida right away for surgery. Thank God for cell phones. Thank God even more for friends like Dr. Keith Hussey. I called Sister a few days after her surgery and asked if she would return to Haiti. She told me that God's goodness to her, especially following the shooting, obliged her to continue to care for the poor of Haiti wholeheartedly. "Besides, we will all die one day anyway. It does not matter how or when or where we die. It only matters how we have lived."

As we were organizing for Sister's emergency care, the phone kept ringing about other kidnapped people and other people shot in areas of conflict. We were back at the Red Planet Market again. This time the special police force was there. I told them I had to go into the slum for an old man who was shot in the abdomen and a young girl shot through the thigh. They told me they could not give me cover. I told them I didn't need cover. They told me I would be killed if I went in. I told them I knew I would not be killed. They asked me why, was I a gangster too? Was I a friend of gangsters? Was I aiding and abetting gangsters? I told them I am a doctor and a priest, and unless they themselves shot me, I knew I would not be shot.

Four of us went in with two stretchers. Eight of us came out. (Aside from the two wounded, two young men offered to help carry the stretchers out.) Not a shot was fired by anyone from the minute we set foot into the slum until we left. When we came out unharmed, the special police gave us a full-scale scrutinizing and search. They were sure we were criminals. We had to be, if we could circulate freely in the slum. They especially searched the two young men that helped us. The police took the pants off of these two to see if they had on women's underwear. Unfortunately, one of them did. It is a sign of being in a gang. When you hide your gun in your waist between your pants and your hip, the extra elastic in women's underwear holds the gun firmly, especially when you run. Wanting to give the benefit of the doubt, I was assuming that this young man must have gone to the wrong clothesline when he got up and dressed before dawn. I don't know how it ended for this "Good Samaritan with a lot of explaining to do." We had to rush the wounded, once more, to the emergency room of Doctors Without Borders.

The next day was my birthday. I worked hard all day caring for the destitute sick at the poorhouse of the Brothers. We rushed to finish early as we were going to play tennis as a foursome in the afternoon. Literally as we began our match, the darn cell phone rang again. It was Sister Marthe. She was frantic. Their jeep driver, another worker, and four of their psychotic patients that were heading to a doctor were kidnapped. I looked at my tennis racket and I heard myself say, "Now, now, Sister. I am sure they will be alright!" I really wanted to play tennis.

Cyrprien, the driver, had a cell phone. Since we have never been able to release kidnapped people immediately anyway, we decided to play out our set, calling the kidnappers on Cyrprien's cell phone whenever the serve changed. On my serve, I was often still on the phone and had to toss and serve with one hand as I roared into the phone. The conversations were complicated by the fact that the kidnappers did not know how to deal with four psychotic kidnapees. This was absolutely no way to play tennis. Of course, we lost.

By the time we had finished playing, we had put pressure on these kidnappers through the Cité Soleil gangs. These kidnappers were outside of Port-au-Prince, in Croix-de-Bouquet. We had finally settled on a moderate sum. Raphael went to finish the arrangement. He called me an hour later. The deal was off. They insisted on a huge payoff. I could not understand what had happened. I went to the convent. It was already dark. No more phone contact was possible with the thugs. So five sisters and five of my mission mates headed to the area. We knew more or less where they were and we would count on God to help us find them.

When we arrive in the dark and deserted place, we found a dead man on the road, head smashed by rocks and arms tied behind him. Not much further up the road was another. We could not figure this out.

A gang of people appeared out of the dark. They told us they are against kidnapping and had killed the people who had kidnapped Cyprien and company. There were their bodies on the road. They gave us Cyprien and Evelyn. The four psychotic patients were at another place and they would give them over the next day. What had happened? The gang leader had gotten nervous by our involvement. He decided to change his spots, and pretend he was a rescuer, not a kidnapper. He killed his first assistant (the one who had agreed to the small payoff by phone). Then he killed his second assistant (the one who demanded an enormous payment). He was trying to save himself by lying, betraying, and murdering his own team. We have seen so many times, always dramatically, how those who serve darkness are devoured by it.

The next morning, as we celebrated the mass in honor of the Assumption of the body of Mary into heaven, the contrast was painfully clear. We are precious to God: heart, mind, body, and soul. Even our bodies are meant by God to be exalted and raised into splendor forever, as was Mary's body. On the other hand, here was the fate of the one who served and was betrayed by darkness: he lay on a deserted road, with bloody and smashed skull and arms bound in slavery to sin, covered with ants, in disgrace. The reign of darkness degrades and destroys, the reign of light exalts and dignifies.

The Beheading of John the Baptist

The end of August brought no quiet. It featured the kidnapping of Jonas (who was raised in our orphanage) and his companion, the kidnapping of Father Wim (a Dutchman) and two companions, and the shooting of Ronsard. Each is quite a story. The story of Fr. Wim is kind of a reverse kidnapping, I was already in the slums calling around and looking around for a man named Lucarne and for a man from New York named Edouard. I could never find Edouard because no one had information about his car. You need to know the vehicle someone was kidnapped in, in order to find the person. Since he is Haitian American from New York, visiting Haiti with no contacts in Haiti, kidnappers used his cell to demand money from his family in New York. The New York family sought help from a local priest who knew me, and that's how I got involved. The family in New York had no information about the car. So we never got him out, and the family in New York was required to pay, probably via Western Union.

I was able to get Lucarne out after 15 days of kidnapping (it took me three days). I paid a very little bit of money, but even that I had to borrow again from the gang. After releasing him, the gang learned that Lucarne was an Aristide protestor, and regretted they had loaned me to money to release him! Jonas was liberated after a day and a half. I had to do it myself. When I got him free he was surprised to see me there among the bandits. He even asked me, "Kisa ki fe ou kap la!" (What makes you able to be in this place?) I think he thought it was me that had kidnapped him!

It was while I was working on releasing the above people that I came across the case of Fr. Wim. He has been in Haiti 35 years. In fact, the gang called ME and asked to come and get him. Fr. Wim had put up such a resistance, it was incredible. He fought non-stop. Imagine a small, white-haired, 65-year-old priest, boxing with the kidnappers. They did not know how to deal with him. Even when I had him safely in the truck, he was still eager to fight. He told me all the things they stole. I demanded everything back and got most of it—in particular, a gold cross his mother gave him after 25 years of being a priest. When the local "boss," whose name is Yoyo Piment, brought the cross, Fr. Wim took another full swing at him. I admired his resistance, but he really didn't know when to quit.

The case of Ronsard is extraordinary. He is a customs broker for us. He has gotten all the containers from Italy out of customs for us—all the equipment for our new hospital. Now we needed him to get out a few containers from Costa Rica, for our electrical installation at our new hospital. He had all the containers out but one. We were in hurry for the last one, since we already have fourteen workers from Costa Rica on site, from the company, to do the electrical installation. A week ago, Ronsard borrowed a car to do this. He was kidnapped, along with the borrowed car. Twelve men who had one gun took him. They shot the gun into the air a number of times to scare him and force him out of the car. When he was out they shot in the air again, but ran out of bullets. Ronsard is a marathon runner and, realizing there was only one gun with no more bullets, he knew he could outrun the twelve, so he ran.

He ran nearly two miles, trying to reach a UN base at an intersection along National Road at Drouillard. The gang, who could not catch him, used the cell phone to call a gang further up the road to stop him. As he neared the UN, the other gang appeared out of the scrublands and shot at him. He was hit in the jaw, his mandible was shattered, the bullet lodged in his throat. He kept running. He collapsed when he reached the UN, and they raced him to a hospital where immediate surgery saved him. We are not sure the surgery was done correctly, in fact we are trying to get him to USA for reevaluation and surgery again if we can, but it did save him. From his recovery bed, with wired jaw and frequent need to spit bloody sputum, he used his cell phone and managed to get our last container out of customs. This is the stuff so many people in Haiti are made of.

A dialogue with Ronsard showed me something that I rarely have time to think about. We see the bullet wounds, the black and blue marks and bruises, but we never can see the damage the kidnapping and violence does to someone inside. To be the victim of violence, to be enslaved, to have your life in the hands of someone evil, to be bartered for like a pig or a dozen mangos. It is sobering and sad to think of the depth of the wounds inflicted by violence, crime and kidnapping. Ronsard told me he wakes up at night, scared and sweating, as he relives what happened to him. I reinforced with him the idea that when things that hit us hard happen in life, we have to see them again and again, because they take time to really enter in and be integrated. But it is equally important to deliberately put a counterbalance. When he wakes up and relives the horror, he should also deliberately relive the blessings: his wise assessment of the situation that made him run, the strong legs and good health that delivered him to UN, the fact that UN raced to help him, the speed and skill of the surgeons, and the visits of friends like us and others who offer solidarity and will pay his hospital bill for him (which is otherwise an enormous burden.) If we don't counterbalance our blows with blessings, we will become closed and cynical about life. Then we are really kidnapped and enslaved, inside, where no one can get us.

The Birth of Mary

The birth of Mary is a concrete sign that the one who will save us is on the way. In fact, Mary is the way. The first light of dawn, called aurora, is the first sign that the sun is on the way. The feast of the birth of Mary, and the first rays of aurora, both promise that something wonderful will soon mark our journey. We just need to wait, and to prepare.

Most sin is the perversion of something good. Hatred is a perversion of love. Jealousy is a perversion of appreciation of differences. Revenge is a perversion of justice. That is why there is hope for us sinners. The basic stuff for something very right is still there, it has just gone very wrong. But it is still there and can be reworked with God's grace. In the end, everything comes down to this: when the heart is perverted there is suffering and death. When the heart is righteous and free there is life, even forever. But how to rework the heart!

Gangs are perversions of families. It is evident that gangs give a feeling of belonging and a feeling of power to the lost and disconnected and powerless. Many of the people that I know in gangs can be led to do the right thing, even at financial loss. What is right in their hearts needs to be recovered. This is hard to do when bitterness and vengeance have built up over the many unspeakable assaults and crimes. Archbishop Desmond Tutu is leading the national reconciliation of South Africa based on this idea. We need to stop, to forgive, and to recover the best of the human heart in everyone.

When I spoke with the five main gang leaders over the past weeks, asking what they thought about Preval's statement that he would kill any bandits that did not disarm, their answer was surprising. They said they agreed, Preval should kill the bandits. They do not see themselves as bandits, but as revolutionaries, trying to better the life of the poor.

Maybe good people always underestimate their goodness, and bad people always underestimate their badness. In the end, everyone has a good measure of both, wild or contained, and to seek ongoing redemption through a long walk with a mysterious God is not a bad goal.

Gandhi's nonviolent way of change the world, was born a hundred years ago today. Terrorists attacked the United States five years ago today, and attack many others around the world every day. The passion for God can unleash angelic or demonic forces. It all depends on us.

Tomorrow is once again slated for disarmament in the slums of Haiti. Let's pray it is a dream that comes true.

Then I can return to being a priest and physician, and abandon my stint as the kidnapper-whisperer.

Fr. Richard Frechette, CP

14

The Thirteenth Day of Christmas

January 7, 2007

The number thirteen can cast a shadow of unease. It represents a kind of thin place, through which evil and harm can slip suddenly into ones life and reap havoc. Christmas cannot be exempt, at least on this side of heaven, from the contradictions crafted by the Prince of Darkness. These twelve days of Christmas had some pretty strong contradictions in them, at least in my very small corner of the world. Feel free to delete them and get on with your life. I wish I could.

"Soldiers," who walk around only with drawn guns, seem to be missing the point. "Gang leaders," who claim to be revolutionaries for a better world via kidnapping and killing, are equally unenlightened (to say the least). But they fire real bullets at each other, using heavy weapons at that, and the real bullets shear real flesh.

In fact, in a heavy holiday gunfire exchange in Cité Soleil, between soldiers and builders of a better world, a young girl took a bullet into the part of her that was "with child." An emergency Cesarean delivered a baby that was dead from a gunshot injury, and the mother still is fighting for her own life. Imagine, shot to death in your mother's womb. The young mother still lies before me in my mind, and I witness her life struggle. The Book of Revelations speaks of a dragon, as big as a third of the sky, whose tail sweeps the very stars away in fury, and who waits eagerly at the side of the pregnant one to devour the fruit of her womb. A fairy tale? I doubt it. And our Church knows that it is no fairy tale, too. Our liturgy shows us blood (red vestments) three times during Christmas week alone: the feasts of St. Stephen, the Holy Innocents, and Thomas Becket. The contradiction to Christmas lives on.

Up the rusty spiral steps, to four more children who got too close to bullets. While asleep on their simple mats, "soldiers" wildly fired shots, long before dawn's early light, hoping to hit the builders of a better world in the dark. What was the result? Blood-soaked mats, the tin roof riddled with bullet holes, with one hole the size of a giant fist. The oldest girl is just 19 years old. Her left shoulder has a gaping wound. She cannot speak from terror. She is still in critical condition. The three younger girls have "lesser wounds": one to the head, one to the arm, and one to the leg. They all have major wounds to the soul. Did anyone notice?

The soldiers deny they shot from the air. The only other explanation is that the four young sisters fired rounds at each other in their sleep, and then shot holes through the roof, and then their guns vanished in thin air. Nowadays, "truth" is whatever the strongest say happened. Maybe it has always been so. Please pray for them—especially the oldest, whose name is Estherline.

On the ninth day of Christmas I met Madame Noel, literally, Mrs. Christmas. I didn't so much meet her as find her on the street, slouched up against a wall, half dead, mouth open and full of flies. We jumped from the truck and picked her up. The stench hit us like a brick wall, and was unmistakable. It was the rotting flesh of cancer. Mrs. Christmas was about 70 years old, and was at the very end of savage, untreated breast cancer, maggots everywhere. Untreated? Yes. She is a sufferer of cancer in a country where poor people have almost no access to health care. In fact, it would be hard for a poor person to find even a daily vitamin.

As we lifted her into the truck, gagging, with the images from Cité Soleil also fresh in my mind, a passerby patted me on the back and said, "Happy New Year, Father." You have got to be kidding. How happiness could have anything to do with all this was utterly beyond me. But I thanked him, smiled, and wished him the same, not realizing the power of the grace present in the timing of his greeting.

Madame Noel never spoke except to say her name. To any question we asked, she would whisper, "Madame Edeline Noel." She seemed to be in a shock similar to that of Estherline, wondering if she was really there, if this was really happening to her. I was completely upside down and feeling lost for the two days that we cared for her. In such situations you feel compassion for what you also abhor. You want to embrace, and you want to run. And your body puts its own brakes on: if you go to near, you retch unceasingly. And it is not lost on Mrs. Christmas, that she is the cause of your retching.

I can understand now the scene in the life of St. Francis where, terrified, he kissed the leper. It was the absolutely courageous and merciful act to bridge the huge gap of such moments, so full of contradiction. I will spare you a detailed description of the wound that spanned her entire chest, and totally destroyed it. When finally and mercifully she died, I prayed over her lifeless body. "May the angels lead you into paradise, may the martyrs rush to welcome you on your way…." As I prayed, I was thankfully given the grace of feeling tremendous satisfaction, and felt myself turning right side up again, and reoriented. There she lay, and that was how she died: in a clean bed, with clean sheets, with clean dressing on her terrible wound, a strong perfume against the stench, IV fluids to keep her from dehydrating, morphine to lessen her agony, and a poinsettia that one of the boys from the orphanage had put on a table next to her bed. Also, she had us as friends: comforting words, daily prayers, and the last sacrament. This beat by far the death she faced on a shabby street in a filthy slum. The passerby was right. Grace will break eagerly into the new year, even if only to give a somewhat happier ending to a disaster, and will wander the earth seeking those willing to give her a chance to do so.

Now we are in our third day trying to release Jayelle from her kidnappers. She is three years old. Her mother is sick with worry and unable to eat or sleep. We spent the feast of the Three Kings trying to release her from criminals who see her only as a cheap trinket that might bring big money, and who promise to give us her head on a platter if we do not comply with their impossible demands. We live in a world where heads have been delivered on platters, with no metaphors involved.

On the feast of the Kings, rather then receiving the gifts that would show her dignity, Jayelle was instead stolen from her bed, in the presence of tied and gagged parents, and has become a dispensable object to be bartered for. On the feast of the Kings, also called the Epiphany (which means "before your face," or "right there in front of you"), we are supposed to be witnessing God's glory made present, not hell's cynical fury. These kidnappings are harder and harder to manage. They are completely out of control, and now involve children—some of whom have been killed. The family already gave their life savings and did not get the child in return. Then they called us to help. So far, we are failing to secure her release, and today is our last chance. But I think we will succeed. Even if we do, the poor family can hardly relocate to another and safer country, but will have to continue living in this same insecure world. And if we don't succeed.... I shudder to think.

Do you remember "A Christmas Carol" by Charles Dickens? Do you remember that Scrooge stood before the ghost of Christmas Present, who opened its cloak and showed two wretched and trembling children? Do you remember their names? They made Scrooge tremble, and they broke his hard heart—so that the real spirit of Christmas could burst into it through the cracks and possess it.

The story I am telling you now is very much Christmas Present. My pen opens the cloak, to me as well as to you. We are not ghosts. It cannot be too late so save humanity, which Christmas reveals to us as also divine.

It is not only Dickens who reaffirms the gospel message. The most striking Christmas card I got this year quotes a Mozarabic text from ninth-century Spain. It says that at Christmas we should not pray for Christ to be born again somewhere else, but rather that the Godhead be grafted into our hearts, here and now. Christ can be conceived in our hearts if we have unquestioning faith, and can abide in us if we keep our spirit free from corruption. Then we will live "overshadowed by the Most High," and be quickened by this power all our days. It's about having the right heart.

Thomas Merton helps us see with more clarity still. He says that when life and death have the same value, which usually means they are both cheap and worth nothing, it is death that spreads like wildfire and dominates over life. This is the contradiction to Christmas.

When life is precious, and death is abhorred—except when it comes at its proper time and represents the fulfillment of life—that is when life spreads like wildfire and dominates over death. This is the conversion of heart that Christmas should represent. Let's pray that it does.

The twelve days of Christmas are over now. The tree lights are off and the wreaths taken down. Ignorance and want still huddle under the mantle of the spirit of the present age. Will you and I dare to be father and mother to them, on the thirteen day of Christmas?

"Happy New Year, Father."

Yes, I believe it can be. If....

Fr. Richard Frechette, CP

15

Crown of Thorns

On the massacre of Alexandra and Stephanie
Cité Soleil, February 1, 2007

like two crowns of thorns
on top of five dry corpses
in final sleep, lay alexandra and stephanie
in the barbaric cave for the dead
known in creole as simply "mog"
my trembling hand blesses them
may the angels lead you far, far from here
and do so in all haste
you and this throng of dead that surround you

their final sleep had not come easily
but followed upon an ideal one
in a shack too small for even a bed
on the floor with mother and father
sleeping securely with naught but love
as their treasure

until shots ring out
no small guns
bullets way too big for small heads
and for the small hearts that suddenly panic
searching for mom with a last gasp

alexandra's eye becomes a deep red canyon, a fjord
and its twin turns to gaze at it
fixed and wide forever
no time for goodbye
only to seek the messenger of light

Into your hands, O Lord, I deliver up my Spirit.
Only you can redeem me, Lord.

stephanie's face shows a quiet peace
but her blood-soaked night wrap
leaves no doubt
of how fast she was gone, unknowingly

mother takes them both in her arms
Precious bundles
And tries to run with them
but to where?
and how?
she finds she cannot move
stayed not by horror
but by her gunshot legs
which become the testament of her steadfast place
in the life and death of her two young gardens
which will never bear fruit

her wailing cannot be consoled
like that a rachel of bethlehem
her lament pierces the world with the terrible news
her children are no more
does anyone really care

i turn to my friend
we are together to offer help
he tries twice but he cannot speak
he is back at his mother's side, a boy again
when so many years ago
hers was also the fate of alexandra
he was ten years old
a gunshot in the night
his mother a pile of brokenness
the wound is fresh
I say
I should have remembered
I am sorry I brought you here
He says simply
You cannot save me from life

another friend sobs heavily
unleashing a flood of sorrow
for children he never knew

soldiers blame the builders of a better world
and the reverse gets equal claim
mother says simply
my children are dead

then she becomes just another news story
and the bodies of her children
become pieces of evidence
and all of humanity grows poorer by light years
never the wiser after eons of the same

stabat mater dolorosa
iuxta crucem lacrimosa
dum pendebant filiae

Fr. Richard Frechette, CP

16

Last Supper in the Shadows

July 20, 2007

The mural of the last supper, just outside the chapel of our children's hospital in Haiti, is intriguing. Most notably, the apostles are represented as children. More subtly, the long shadows cast by sunset are depriving half the children of light.

Even though there were no children at the Last Supper, truth is well represented here. Children are no strangers to the paschal mystery of suffering. Nature, who has her own way of speaking through signs, is making her own point. Far too many children in the world live in the shadows of hunger, sickness, poverty, prostitution, slavery, homelessness, and war. They are deprived of light.

I have commented before that, when the political situation is quieter in Haiti, we see the suffering around us with more focus. After nearly seven years of unbearable violence, Haiti has been relatively peaceful this year. Strong initiatives by the UN and police have seen the arrest of many gang members. The leaders we were used to rubbing shoulders with are either dead or in prison. By the same token, swarms of unsettled and unemployed young men will probably not stay leaderless for long. But for now there is peace on the street.

The story is often very different in our hospital, where peace is often disturbed by suffering. Recently, we got to know a heroic mother, who sat at the bedside of her baby boy for 38 straight days. Late at night, you would see her slumped over the crib, on a hard wooden chair, her eyes fixed on her beloved child, Daniel. It was a sight as sad as it was inspiring—like a sunrise and sunset at the same time. This mom believed that if she left the bedside, her child would die. She believed if she took her eyes off of him for a minute, he would die. So she would do anything, and bear any suffering, to keep him alive, by keeping him in her sight and in her heart.

His death was a mortal blow to her. We would do well to pause now, and keep her in *our* sight through prayer, and in our heart through compassion. She highly deserves our efforts to be spiritually close to her. She is a great woman brought low by terrible loss.

In the Bible, prayer is often seen as begging for God to remember us, to keep us in sight. It can't go well for us when God's gaze is somewhere else. The fear is that out of sight really does means out of mind. We would fall out of existence altogether if we were no longer in God's thoughts. Even though it took too literal a meaning in her understanding, that mom was onto something very true, and she fought her son's death with all her might, with her vision. She fought it with her eyes, the pristine windows of the soul. Death cannot negate the steadfastness and faithfulness of love. Love is stronger than death. It is the greatest of the only three things that will last.

A small boy named Rene has known his share of suffering. He has the disease of our age, HIV/AIDS. His mother died of it years ago. He is an orphan from our home. If he looks well in spite of his illness, it is no little thanks to a lady who visits him constantly and loves him as her own. Catarina's heart is filled with love for him, and she pours it out in good measure, overflowing. His head is bandaged because of terribly infected wounds. His disease is taking him slowly. A picture of the two of them together a joy to see. It shows heaven is breaking through the darkness of tragedy, like a glorious sunrise." This is my beloved son, on whom my favor rests."

Just yesterday, his "godmother" Catarina took Rene to the chapel. He was in great pain, and very forlorn. Together they looked at the wounds in the hands of St. Francis, and then the wounded head of Christ (wounds very similar to his own.) It is strange, but somehow this boy gained a profound understanding when he saw those images.

This understanding helped him, and although it is not easy to express the reason in words, it has to do with forming a friendship with God, which can mysteriously flourish with suffering. This is because of God's longing to be with those suffering the most, a longing often expressed in the Bible. The worse the suffering, the stronger God's longing. A child surely can have mystical awareness.

Sometimes Rene and Catarina join us after mass, when we bathe and anoint the children who have died during the night, and wrap them for burial. He is curious and yet frightened, and is trying to cure himself of the fear that when he dies he will be taken away by zombies. I caught him looking at me, wide-eyed, as we finished our ritual, and so I said to him, "Imagine! A sign of the cross and a prayer can protect us from evil, and give us all the strength we need." Then his eyes strayed to our child coffins, made of papier-mâché. I broke his trance by showing him a big one. "This is my favorite. Be sure to put me in this one when it's my turn to go to God!" His simple giggle put death at bay.

To put it simply, another child, named Fhito, is turning into plastic, inside and out. He enjoys the visits of his dad while he can. His circulation is failing, and he is getting deep infections. His skin and nerves are tightening like drums. He doesn't say much, but when he does, it is with a very soft voice. He cannot know what is happening to him, or where life is leading him. While we cringe at his suffering, he is going to his destiny patiently, like an innocent lamb.

"Look, Oh Lord, and see my suffering! Come quickly to my aid." This is the cry of tenebrae (shadows), from the Christian Liturgy of the Hours, remembering the Passion of Jesus on Good Friday. The chant of the monks is beautiful, but there is also something holy about a card game. Jean has such bad cancer; it takes huge amounts of morphine to control his pain. He can't eat solid food anymore because of the cancer, but luckily he likes ice cream, and milkshakes, and his mom, and me, and Conan, and Kyra, and life. He loves to talk, and carries on as if he has a hundred years ahead of him. And he plays a mean game of cards!

Life is not fair. But what can we do?

We can be faithful to those whose sufferings are difficult, and steadfastly show them friendship. We can give witness to faith, hope and love, which are deep human values and spiritual treasures, and the only three things that will last. What can we do? Nothing and everything.

"In the tender compassion of our God,
the dawn from on high will break upon us-
To shine on those who dwell in darkness and the shadow of death,
And to guide out feet into the way of peace."

Fr. Richard Frechette, CP

17

Fr. Bill Wasson Remembered, for Forever and a Day

Founder of Nuestros Pequeños Hermanos
August 26, 2007

In ancient times, if someone were missing for a year and a day, they were declared officially dead, lost to the world. A year and a day meant gone forever.

We have gone through a full year's cycle now, without Fr. Bill:

Without his humor, his enthusiasm,

without his challenge and advice-

without his wisdom, his surprises-

Without his travels (how the airline industry must have suffered this past year!),

Without his meals and masses.

It might seem that he is farther from us now than ever, as the ancient custom would state.

But for us who are believers, the year has also been a liturgical year of renewal, of deepening, of reliving abiding mysteries. The Advent season taught us again to keep our hope strong, even when we cannot see what we hope for. Christmas taught us how close

God is to us … even sharing our human blood, our human heart. (Our hearts now can beat with God and for God, to transform the world.) The reality of suffering and the love of sacrifice were dramatically evident throughout Lent and Holy Week. And the risen Christ shows us that nothing valuable to God is ever lost, not our spirits, nor our souls, nor even our wounds. (Fr. Bill sure had his share of those.)

Before a year and a day could pass, in fact just shy one day, we staged a protest against the thinking of the world. Anniversary masses were celebrated for Fr. Bill at all our homes, on August 16. They were our deliberate attempt to show that he is present in our hearts and in our thinking, and in the mystery of God. We believe that the "Church in heaven," the company of the faithful who have died, are united with us," the Church on earth," and that we make up one mystical body in Christ. We commune with those who have gone before us through prayer, and their spirits are very much present to us and influential in our lives. Fr. Bill's spirit is not at all lost to the world—especially not to us.

It is worth noting that during the years before Christ died, his disciples showed remarkable weakness. They were, as we know, simple people of no special training: fishermen, tax collectors, and the like. They were sometimes ill-tempered, ill-mannered, and plain wrong in their attitudes and thinking. Christ frequently challenged them publicly for this. When things got very painful and dangerous for Christ, and they had to "stand up and be counted," they were scared to death and ran for their lives.

Yet these same men were, strangely, quite something else after Christ died. Everything he had ever told them, any lesson he ever taught them, somehow became more fully understood than ever before. Now they saw his teachings as bold and dynamic truths. The example he had given them, over and over by his own life, came back to them with brilliant conviction. These timid, ordinary men, who were afraid for their skins, suddenly were guided by a force that carried them valiantly into the future and into the world. They became fully servants of the gospel of life: articulate, fearless, leading by example, traveling far and wide to spread the Word, even at great danger to themselves. They had formerly been afraid. Now they were willing to shed their blood while doing the work of God. Many of them did.

What changed them? What made the difference? Simply put, the Spirit of Christ was even more present to them, more powerful in their lives, after his death than during his life. And this made all the difference in the world, and to the world.

We have had a year to adjust to carrying out our mission without Fr. Bill, as the mission becomes ever larger, ever more complex, ever more needed in our world—and very much in need of keeping a strong spirit, and a right heart.

Fr. Bill's spirit was strong and effective while he was alive, because he united it with the Spirit of the Risen Christ. His energy, intuition, wisdom and achievements came from his priestly openness to the will of God. This union is exactly what makes his spirit available to us today.

Our best way of remembering Fr. Bill, our best way of maintaining his spirit, our best way of serving the mission he began and the children entrusted to us, is to do as he did: to pray, to trust God, and to act in faith.

Let's pray together that, just as the disciples had more strength and momentum for mission after the death of Christ (even because of his death), that our energy and enthusiasm and commitment to Fr. Bill's mission increase in us with every passing year.

Rather than forgetting Fr. Bill after a year and a day, he will be remembered forever and a day. May he rest in peace.

Fr. Richard Frechette, CP

18

Assumption into Earth
(On the Burial of Hundreds
of Destitute Dead)

August 15, 2007

Birthday
and the vigil of the great feast
Rounding the bend for the 54th time
Still trotting strongly
time again for a dozen full moons
the span between each ever shorter

and for 365 more full strides
Through sunshine and shadow (and no little fog)
Into some nasty places
where only God's Sistine touch can save
And yet other places so wondrous
They call out only for deep thanks and praise
(Lord it is good for us to be here)

Contrasts
To celebrate birth by burying the dead
Today, two hundred and ninety one
of the too many forgotten dead
Whose poverty hounds them even after death
Many are babes and children
Who never had my chance, or yours
Nameless now (not to God)
Faceless now (nature saw to that)
Brought out into daylight by a daughter of St Francis
Like a mother of 291 sorrows
Pieta
A young man helps us
Not noticing much the meaning of what he is doing
Just that it needs to be done

Brought out from these caves which keep the dead
Where they waited, one atop another.
The Last Judgment (which has to be better than this)
Like piles of (less than) manure

A vision from God
Let there be for them a garden
A place in warm earth
Under wild grass
Kissed by the strong sun
Where one awaits the last things in wild beauty
If wait we must

We take them there
We plant them like seeds
Cigarettes help against gagging

Rum helps even more
"I'll have a rum and smoke"
And once in place
We softly tread above them
With our incense and holy water
And the sound of music
of trumpet and a few big drums
First dirges
Then joyful noise
Announcing the end of exodus and exile
(May their souls and the souls of all the departed rest in peace)

Warriors of light
Warriors of prayer
To do the right is truly a battle
Much of it, but not all, with oneself
The Holy Mother is taken to heaven
The head of the serpent is crushed
(the prince of the forces that oppose God in hate)
But the venom persists, and will poison us still
until we understand
That our Mother is restless for all her children
(not just the lucky)
And that burying the dead in the good earth
Is also an assumption into higher realms.

Fr. Richard Frechette, CP

19

St. Nicholas and the Antichrist

December 6, 2007

HOW BEAUTIFUL UPON THE MOUNTAINS ARE THE FEET of the one who brings good tidings, who proclaims peace; who brings the good news of salvation; who announces to Zion, You God reigns! (Isaiah 52:7)

St. Nicholas surely had this kind of feet. His pilgrim journeys not only gladdened the heart of humanity in his day, but his reputation was so great that it has carried his name forward for 1,700 years, to our own day.

Certainly, the centuries have changed him. The bishop's miter that graced his head has flopped over and gained white trim, his red bishop robes have turned into an oversized pantsuit, and a thousand generations of use have slurred his name into "Santa Claus." But unlike many saints whose popularity is confined to a region or a country, St. Nicholas is one of the few saints known and loved in almost all the world. Even in his secular form, he represents wisdom, kindness and generosity, as should any present day successor of the apostles, known to us as bishops.

St. Nicholas was able to live out a vibrant and hopeful message in a time of great suffering, controversy and confusion. The gladness of his news, when contrasted with very dark human experiences of his day, is like a bright star in the black velvet, midnight sky.

Our Christian tradition makes no denial of darkness, not even when the extra lights of the holidays do their best to make the darkness vanish in an artificial way. Sometimes the darkness we must fight is inside where Christmas tree lights can never reach.

Recently, in the vast Port-au-Prince slum called Cité Soleil, a sickly young woman asked me to help her. Her name was Solange. She was so small and slight; I was surprised when she told me she was in her twenties. When I listened to her heart, the gushy murmurs made me picture her heart valves as thick, shredded sponges. I was sure she had valve damage from previous rheumatic fever, which is still very prevalent here. A cardiologist friend confirmed this and thought surgery was still possible, so I arranged for Solange to go to the Dominican Republic for surgery.

A few days after Solange left, we had bad rains, then terrible rains, then worse rains still, and then a full-stop flood. We went into high gear, helping thousands of flooded neighbors get out of the water to shelter. While in the midst of all the flood chaos, I got a call from the Dominican Republic saying that Solange had died during the night. They didn't know what to do with her body or how to let her family in Haiti know that she was dead.

So we handled a disaster within a disaster, using cell phones during flood relief to arrange the return of Solange's body to Haiti by airplane, and to call the family to come to find us in the floods so we could give the news personally and not by phone.

My head started to spin. The family will probably blame us

for her death. They will want money. They will say I should have left her alone, that the trip was too tiring for her. When the body comes on the plane it will difficult getting the body through immigration. They will need to be bribed. The family will want us to pay for the funeral, etc, etc, etc....

Fatigue, frustration, and cynicism know how to twist the mind and heart. They are the weapons of the Antichrist.

Having worked myself up into an angry and defensive posture, when the family asked us to drive the body all the way to Thiotte (a six-hour drive), I recited in full-voice a list of everything we had already done for Solange, and what it cost in terms of money and effort. Soon the force of my words started to fade. There was her body, in front of me, in a simple coffin. There had been no problems at immigration, no bribes to pay. Just compassionate officials who helped things move rapidly for the grieving family of paupers. I realized with embarrassment that I should be using my mouth for blessing her body, for praying for her family standing before me in their grief, and not for my unsolicited defense. The family was kind and understanding. No demands. No blame. They were only asking for a ride to Thiotte with a dead body, what was left of someone they dearly loved. If we couldn't help, they would try to manage another way.

Then I was completely caught off guard. The family told me they were going home to Thiotte because their simple home in Port au Prince was destroyed by the water and mud of the floods, and they had no place to go with Solange. They had no place but home, in Thiotte. Their life was all loss. Then, they thanked me for sending Solange to the Dominican Republic. If she hadn't gone, they said, she would have had a terrible death in the water and mud.

Who had the sicker heart? Me or Solange? How did St. Nicholas, and so many great people through the ages, keep the right heart in the face of danger and stress and disaster? They had a special gift, a keen intelligence as to what was really happening inside people and in their true situations, that could not be blunted or distorted by preconceptions or habits of response based on fatigue or cynicism. They had personality and situation intelligence. What a great gift to ask for at Christmas, from the real Santa Claus—a keen, intelligent heart.

Esmine was kidnapped last Thursday. Yes, it is all starting up again. After coming out of the bank with a good bit of money to pay for the schooling of her three young children, she was grabbed by strangers and gone. How? Had someone inside the bank tipped off the ones outside? Was she betrayed? Days passed, negotiating with kidnappers for money the family did not have. They were threatening to kill her. These are not idle threats, as two kidnapped children had been killed during the past ten days. I put up half the ransom for Esmine. I even went to do the drop off for the kidnappers. "Leave the money at the third telephone pole, on the left, after the bridge."

How I despised what the kidnappers were doing, when I remembered the children that were killed by them and how they died, when I thought of Esmine's distress and her distraught children at home. I even felt anger against Esmine, for getting kidnapped in the first place and somehow pulling me into it. I wanted to hide out by the pole and beat them when they came for the money. "Lord, keep our hearts from becoming like those of our oppressors!" It really is all about heart, a struggle with darkness in the heart.

Esmine was released at four in the morning, and came to see me at the hospital right away. She had been beaten, she was humiliated, and she was full of fear of the streets, of society, of the future. She rolled on the ground in front of me, crying out her grief, but also sputtering out words of thanks for our help in freeing her. I couldn't get her to stand up, and I didn't have the heart to look at her on the ground so defeated, so I looked to the sky above. The moon was a bright crescent, but its full round border was made visible by the aurora of the far off sun. And, to the left of the crescent in all its glory, was the morning star.

I understood immediately. The moon was Esmine. Her glory, her Godlight, was diminished by the dark evil of her captivity and humiliation, but it was faintly still there. The crescent was the part of her that still had light, and somehow promised a healing light for the remaining silhouette. God was the aurora, the sun underneath and unseen, a subtle light illuminating Esmine's wound that could be healed by hope. And the morning star? That's the best part. The morning star is you, and me, and anyone, anywhere, at any while, who stands in solidarity with the one who is in darkness and the shadow of death to offer even imperfect or limited light. This gift of light is antidote to the Antichrist.

You can't believe how hard it is to bury the dead. No one wants them. We bury about 100 a week. Their poverty and humiliation still hound them after they are dead. Their disgraceful condition, their lack of a place even to drop dead on, their exile from a final resting place, are haunting realities. When we recently brought a score of these destitute to their final resting place last week, we were met with a posse of peasants who demanded money and would not let us pass to the twenty graves we had dug. There was quite a fight between my team, who were there to manage all the coffins and the graves, and the peasants who insisted they could make a fortune on that land by saving it for a cell-phone company antenna. They insisted their deal with the company was getting ruined by our bones.

I knew it was State land. I knew the dead have been dumped there for 30 years. But I had no energy left to fight and I called for the gravediggers, the team of 20 pallbearers, and all the coffins to go to a place in Cité Soleil the mayor said we could have for funerals, but which we had not yet prepared for lack of resources. My team refused to leave and wanted to defend the dead. The small music band that always comes to play for the funerals (I call them the "other" grateful dead) struck up a lively tune. The fight was on. The police soon came, and went to the highest bidder ... which was me. Yes, I could outdo the protesting peasants—gas money, a little money for lunch, a little extra for Christmas. We won. The dead now rested in peace.

The human heart beats in darkness, against darkness, and easily becomes darkness. But it longs for light, true light. At Christmas we celebrate the presence of a new heart beating among us. Small at first, but over a very few years it grows in strength, wisdom and grace. If we want, this sacred heart beats first next to ours, then with ours, and then in ours. Each beat generates light, the true light that the darkness cannot overcome. Darkness loses its power, and falls from its throne as seeming victor. It becomes simply "opponent." Even its opposition is self-defeating, since it only increases longing for the Sacred Heart, whose power and light we come to share. This power and light reveal His name, but we find we have always known it. His name is "Wonderful, Counselor, Almighty God, Everlasting Father, Prince of Peace."

May it be ever in our hearts and on our lips.

Fr. Richard Frechette, CP

20

The Land of Milk and Honey

July 11, 2008

I wondered what the bees were doing there. A normal person would wonder what the dead man was doing there. It's amazing what you get used to.

But there he was, propped upright in his open coffin, leaning against the vandalized grave. He was pretty nearly a skeleton, though his suit was rather well preserved. A swarm of bees danced all around his head, content but not far from menacing. Their frenetic flights to and from their macabre honeycomb, and their loud heavy droning, put me off from my first instinct to close the lid and push him back into his grave with a quick, stingless blessing.

But I remembered what it was like so many years ago, as a novice beekeeper in the monastery, when on a wintry day I tried to give the bees their sugar water, the seasonal substitute for flowers. I slipped on the ice, the jar fell and jolted them, and I couldn't make a quick getaway because of the icy ground and my long black robes. Thirty some stings later, mostly on my frostbitten head, I was free from their attack. An angry bee is an angry bee, in the dead of a Baltimore winter or here in the heat of the tropics.

Another huge drone sounded overhead. An American Airlines jet passed above, seemingly almost at arm's length, as it traced the final quarter-mile of its journey from Miami to Port-au-Prince. It is an hour and a half journey, but a world away.

I pictured the people in the plane above—a score of missionaries, a handful of deportees, not a few business people, and many home-comers. How many would scratch below the surface of what it is really happening here, East of Eden, where poverty and violence give a poisonous fruit from the tree of death.

So, the peasants had seen the bees entering and leaving the grave through a small crack. They knew it meant honey. Can you imagine being that desperate for honey that you think nothing of disturbing a dead man's rest, and scraping the honeycomb from his coffin?

Do dead men really tell no tales?

They tell of hunger, of revolutions that happen for simple food and water. "Let them eat honey." They tell of magic and mystical beliefs, where honey from the grave is manna from the realm between the dead and the living.

In front of the coffin is a makeshift hive. This is about the only normal and redeeming part of the image: the attempt to attract the queen, and thereby the whole swarm, into the normal way of sharing human company.

I offered to come with another, honey-free coffin and bury that man (for a second time.) "Can't you see he doesn't need to be buried? He is just bones for burning."

The bees started with death and ended with something sweet. A strange image for strange times, but it oddly speaks of something timeless. Flowers are as rare in poverty as they are in winter.

The riddle of Samuel: out of the killer, something to eat. Out of the dead, something sweet. History has its cycles.

There are other forms of death that are worse than "our sister, death of the body": the death of the will to live, the death of hope, the death of joy. This kind of death turns people into walking dead.

I have a friend named Semares. I stopped to see him recently. His once bright eyes are empty now. They say lightening never strikes twice in the same place, but it isn't true.

When he was a boy, begging on the streets, he got caught in gunfire and lost his leg. But he rebounded, and refused to accept his limitation. How he used to hop and jump into my truck when we pass by, swift as a deer, bright white teeth forming a quarter-moon smile! Believe it or not, he formed a team of one-legged soccer players—he proudly carries their picture with him! And they are a force to be reckoned with.

About six weeks ago, a truck lost its breaks. Semares was in the crowd. His good leg was crushed, his belly ripped open. Everyone who was around him at the moment, as he later described it, had to be scraped up with shovels. As the lone survivor, he told me "God saved me because I never once told a lie." He looked at me with no expression, without a smile, with no light in his eyes. How do we, his friends, light his heart again? Can we catch the light for him? I wish I could pass him what's left of my own.

Felix is upstairs as I write this. I don't know him; I only know that he needs a Good Samaritan. He needs friendship and trust and prayers and a lot of time to heal. Felix was kidnapped about 10 days ago, and when he could come up with no money for ransom, he was very badly beaten and thrown into a cesspool to drown. Who can doubt hell's fury? His jaw has been rebuilt and wired. Not to worry. We bought gallons of Ensure (a liquid nutrient) and fruit juices for him—and plenty of straws. It will be a long time before he can eat.

His eyes are also empty. Is there any wonder why? Setting bones is the easy part. Trying to restore light to the soul is the most difficult of arts.

Yes, who can doubt hell's fury? Who can doubt how poverty and violence can tear the hope, joy and life out of people?

But who can doubt heaven's thunder?

The booming protests against those who would humiliate and disgrace the image of God in the human heart!

Who can doubt the power of heaven's light, a light sometimes beaten to weakness and submission, feeble in the darkness, and nearly gone—but which, St. John promises, may spend a season as ember, but it will spark and reignite and burn brightly, never to be overcome? "The light shone in the darkness, and the darkness was not able to overcome it."

Who can doubt the heavenly strength, clearly present in those who seem so weak, yet manage to keep going against all odds?

Who can doubt the power that heaven gives to you and me, the lucky and the strong, to redress the wrong, and restore the inner light of joy?

Yes, to the east, in the Garden of Eden, there is an angel, with a flaming sword guarding the way to the tree of life. The foe will perish; the friend will pass. The land of milk and honey is just a flaming sword away.

Fr. Richard Frechette, CP

Conclusion

When the world that surrounds us is in chaos, from violence, natural disasters, poverty, and the ensuing degeneration, the mind and heart are in danger of gravitating toward an internal chaos that absorbs and perpetuates the outer. The pillars on which a sound mind and heart rest begin to crumble.

However, among others, there are three important pillars for inner health. These include feeling secure and that life is overall predictable, feeling important and that life overall has a purpose, and feeling worthy and that overall life is welcoming. These are basic needs, and much disease (personal and social) is generated whenever one lives in dangerous situations without power, consistently experiences life as absurd, and lives with a feeling of inferiority and shame. The ancient scourges of the human family—poverty, ignorance, sickness, and violence—assault human well-being on all three fronts.

The world's religions and philosophies have offered balms and salves to ease the wounds that come from existential anxiety. Inner chaos can lead to insanity, addictions, and despair. It can lead to irrational and destructive behaviors, to murder and suicide.

Christianity has offered its own solutions to these crises, proposing that there is a spiritual fullness available to all people at all moments, even in the toughest of circumstances, and that there is an inner goodness in people that can respond to this fullness with a saving effect. Christianity proposes that in the face of the existential fears, there are existential truths that can keep us floating upright as we navigate difficult seas toward better times.

We are destined for greatness. We have a triple dignity: God made us, redeemed us and prepares us for life eternally. This is our supreme security. Even though we may know the sufferings and sorrows of the way of a cross, our wounds are part of a cosmic redemption story, in which we play an intimate part. Christianity proposes that we are given life uniquely and deliberately by God, and that we have an essential place in the drama of sharing space and time together, finitely, on a journey to forever. Though we suffer humiliations and indignities through desperate situations, or through violence, Christianity proposes that we are made in the Divine image, held by God's hand, considered as the apple of God's eye, with every hair of our head counted, and our names engraved in God's heart. These propositions can be hard to hold onto in the crucible, but Christianity has persistently and bravely held them up as banners and standards of truth throughout the ages.

As surely as the human body applies awesome energies to rebuild and regenerate itself after being sick or wounded, the human soul (seat of emotion, intellect and life force) applies amazing energies to keeping oneself righted and steady on a path toward life. The reflections contained in this book are true stories of magnificent people who, sailing the stormy seas of chaos, have known the power of faith.

Of interest to humanists and anthropologists, to philosophers and theologians, is the instinct, in the face of adversity, not just to survive, but to thrive with passion and flair. This instinct opens a way to know a God of tough places, a Lord of those tragically burned by the fires of life. Real? Imaginary? Revelation? Poetry?

Your heart will let you know.